THE VEGETARIAN ATHLETE'S COOKBOOK

Bloomsbury USA
An imprint of Bloomsbury Publishing Plc

1385 Broadway   50 Bedford Square
New York   London
NY 10018   WC1B 3DP
USA   UK

www.bloomsbury.com

BLOOMSBURY and the Diana logo are trademarks of Bloomsbury
Publishing Plc

First published 2017

Photography by Adrian Lawrence
Food styling by Emily Kydd
Design and illustrations by Louise Turpin

ISBN: PB: 978-1-63286-643-1

ebook: 978-1-63286-644-8

LIBRARY OF CONGRESS CATALOGING-IN-PUBLICATION DATA IS AVAILABLE

2 4 6 8 10 9 7 5 3 1

Typeset in Myriad Pro by Sunrise Studios

Printed and bound in China by C&C Offset Printing Co., Ltd.

Bloomsbury Publishing Plc makes every effort to ensure that the papers
used in the manufacture of our books are natural, recyclable products
made from wood grown in well-managed forests. Our manufacturing
processes conform to the environmental regulations of the country of
origin.

To find out more about our authors and books visit www.bloomsbury.com.
Here you will find extracts, author interviews, details of forthcoming events
and the option to sign up for our newsletters.

Bloomsbury books may be purchased for business or promotional use.
For information on bulk purchases please contact Macmillan Corporate and
Premium Sales Department at specialmarkets@macmillan.com.

THE VEGETARIAN ATHLETE'S COOKBOOK

MORE THAN 100 DELICIOUS RECIPES FOR ACTIVE LIVING

ANITA BEAN

B L O O M S B U R Y

NEW YORK · LONDON · OXFORD · NEW DELHI · SYDNEY

CONTENTS

INTRODUCTION

"**Y**ou can't build muscle without meat!" is the typical reaction I get when I tell people that I'm a vegetarian athlete and competed as a bodybuilder for 10 years before winning the British Bodybuilding Championships in 1991. Most look at me in disbelief. "Surely you need meat to compete?" No way. My trophy may have gathered a bit of dust over the years ago, but it is solid proof that you can gain significant muscle and make it to the top of your sport without meat.

Whether you are already a committed vegetarian, are thinking of giving up meat, or simply fancy having one or two meat-free days a week, I hope that this book will inspire you to try something new and show you that—contrary to popular belief—you can build muscle without meat. Indeed, eating less meat is a fast-growing trend. According to a 2014 YouGov survey for Eating Better, one in five people have cut back on meat in the past year and one in three are considering eating less meat. For many people, eating less meat is an easier option than giving it up completely.

Although the number of vegetarians has remained more or less static over the past ten years, at around 3 percent of the population, there has been a significant rise in the number of flexitarians—people who eat mostly vegetarian food but occasionally eat meat.

People are cutting out meat for many reasons, including concerns about health, animal exploitation and animal welfare, sustainability, and climate change. Recent decades have seen the meat consumption of rich countries increase, causing dangerously high levels of pollution and greenhouse gas emissions, an unprecedented rise in global temperature, widespread deforestation and loss of plant and animal species, and adding unnecessary pressure to already strained resources.

One of my aims in writing this book is to dispel the myths surrounding vegetarian diets. There is plenty of proof that a vegetarian diet is healthier than a typical meat-eater's diet. It's also better for the environment, more sustainable, a better use of land, and a good way of cutting your carbon footprint. Livestock farming generates huge amounts of greenhouse gases, which are major contributors to global warming and pollution. It also uses vast amounts of freshwater and is a grossly inefficient use of land. By eating less meat, you will be helping to protect the environment. For me, not eating meat is also an ethical choice; I don't think animals should be exploited. The truth is we don't need to eat meat to be healthy.

Until now, I've not preached to anyone about not eating meat. Like politics and religion, the issue of meat eating often touches on people's core ethical and moral values, which can be hard to change. But when people ask why I don't eat meat then I'm happy to explain. My choice not to eat it was born partly from habit (my parents were vegetarian so I was brought up without meat) and an abhorrence of animal suffering, as well as a genuine dislike of the stuff. Although I never had to give up Sunday roasts or bacon, the idea of eating animals really doesn't appeal.

There's no denying that it was difficult being a vegetarian child growing up in the 60s and 70s. I was the only one who didn't eat meat at my school; school dinners were a nightmare. I was given a plate of grated cheese or hard-boiled eggs instead of the meat that all the other kids were eating. I was a pooper at birthday parties because I wouldn't eat the sausage rolls. I was a "problem" when invited to friends' houses for tea ("what, you don't like fish sticks?"). No one could understand why I wouldn't eat meat in those days.

Nowadays, of course, being vegetarian is a lot more acceptable socially and far easier to explain when eating out. My own children have plenty of delicious veggie options at school like lentil lasagna and Mediterranean pasta bake. When they visit friends, they don't have to apologize for being vegetarian. When I go out to eat, there's usually at least one or two dishes on the menu that don't contain meat. And supermarkets are now full of exciting vegetarian foods. Life has become so much easier!

Although my competitive days are over, I've endeavored to help other vegetarian athletes succeed in sports. They include my own two daughters who are both competitive swimmers and train for more than 18 hours a week. They've never eaten meat, yet, over the years, have managed to enjoy success at county, regional, and national level.

In this book, I explain how a vegetarian diet can help you succeed in your sport or activity, which foods you need to focus on, how to avoid the common pitfalls of a vegetarian diet, and how you can put a vegetarian diet into practice. I've devised more than 100 healthy and delicious recipes for breakfasts, main meals, soups, salads, desserts, snacks, smoothies, and shakes. Every recipe is designed to meet the needs of active people and athletes. They are all packed with fresh, nutritious ingredients so you know you'll be getting the right combination of nutrients to help you perform better, build muscle, and promote recovery and health. Best of all, they are all incredibly easy to make, require minimal cooking skills, and taste amazing.

Bon appetit!

PART 1

Vegetarian Sports Nutrition Guide

CHAPTER 1

WHY NO MEAT?

BENEFITS OF A VEGETARIAN DIET

Many people think vegetarianism is just a fad. Well, they couldn't be more wrong. Vegetarianism encompasses a lot more than not eating meat. It is a lifestyle, a state of mind, a set of inherent beliefs and values that are unique and important to each individual. The list of reasons why people choose not to eat meat is varied and includes issues relating to the environment, economy, religion, ethics, animal welfare, compassion, and, of course, health.

Sustainability has become a major issue and there are now real fears that, if current trends in meat consumption continue, we will not be able to feed the world's expanding population. Meat production is a highly inefficient use of land, water, and energy compared with growing plants. There are currently 7.2 billion people in the world and the population is predicted to rise to 9.6 billion by 2050, according to the United Nations. People are living and eating longer. This means we must somehow make the earth's resources stretch to feed all these people, and for a longer time period. It has been estimated that 50–70 percent more food must be produced by 2050. The time is now to make small changes that can make a big impact on our planet. There is a very simple solution to many of the world's greatest problems, and it starts with eating less meat. A vegetarian diet requires far fewer environmental resources, such as energy, land, pesticides, chemical fertilizer, fuel, feed, and water, than a meat-based diet, and is undoubtedly more sustainable (Pimentel & Pimentel, 2003; Berners-Lee et al., 2012; Carbon Trust, 2015). Here are nine reasons to make the transition to a plant-based diet.

DEFINITION OF VEGETARIAN DIETS

LACTO-OVO VEGETARIAN:
The most common type of vegetarian diet, which includes both dairy products and eggs.

LACTO VEGETARIAN: Includes dairy products but not eggs.

OVO VEGETARIAN: Includes eggs but not dairy products.

VEGAN: Excludes all foods and products of animal origin, including honey.

FLEXITARIAN: Also referred to as "semi-vegetarian" or "part-time vegetarian," a mostly vegetarian diet with meat and fish consumed occasionally.

PESCATARIAN (or **PESCO VEGETARIAN**): Avoids meat but includes fish, seafood, eggs, and dairy products.

NOTE: Flexitarian and pescatarian are a bit of an oxymoron, but you will come across people who use these terms to describe their eating habits.

1 IT'S BETTER FOR THE ENVIRONMENT

Few people are aware of the link between climate change, diet, and meat consumption. However, livestock farming (therefore meat consumption) is the leading cause of greenhouse gas emissions. Everyone thinks that climate change and global warming are due to burning fossil fuels but livestock farming is responsible for 51 percent of greenhouse gas emissions from human-related activities, which is considerably more than the entire transport sector (Goodland & Anhang, 2009). Switching to a vegetarian or vegan diet could cut out those emissions by 70 percent and 63 percent respectively (Spingman et. al., 2016).

Greenhouse gas emissions include carbon dioxide (from fossil fuels used to power farm machinery and to transport, store, and cook foods), nitrous oxide (released from fertilized soils), and methane (from enteric fermentation in ruminant livestock). Due to their unique digestive process, cows, sheep, and other ruminant livestock generate substantial amounts of methane, which is 25 times more potent than carbon dioxide. A single cow produces between 66 to 132 gallons of methane a day.

We are already perilously close to the maximum 2°C rise in global temperatures agreed in 2010 by member states at the UN climate change conference in Cancun. Unless we switch to a more sustainable plant-based diet, greenhouse gas emissions from food production will make it extremely difficult to keep below this limit (Bajželj et al., 2014). Scientists say that, if this 2°C limit is exceeded, we will see widespread extinction of animal and plant species, droughts, deforestation, a rise in sea level, an increased risk of flooding of low-lying areas near the coast, and even the total submergence of low-lying islands. In other words, global warming will have a devastating impact on our planet.

So how can we keep the temperature rise below 2°C? Eating less meat is an obvious strategy. If adopted worldwide, it would generate a quarter of the emissions reductions we need to keep below this level by 2015, according to a report from Chatham House, the Royal Institute of International Affairs (Wellesley et al., 2015). This echoes the recommendation by the Carbon Trust, which also says that moving towards more vegetarian eating will dramatically reduce the impact on the environment (Carbon Trust, 2015). In other words, cutting meat will increase the sustainability of our diet and feed the world more fairly and humanely.

■ More than a third of all raw materials and fossil fuels consumed in the US are used in animal production.

■ The production of one calorie of animal protein requires more than ten times the fossil fuel input as a calorie of plant protein.

■ A person who follows a plant-based diet produces 50 percent less CO_2 and uses $1/11$th oil, $1/13$th water, and $1/18$th land.

■ Cutting out meat can cut your carbon footprint by 50 percent.

■ Fertilizer spread on soil generates nitrous oxide, which is 300 times more damaging to the climate than carbon dioxide.

■ Greenhouse gas emissions in meat-eaters are approximately twice as high as those in vegans (Scarborough et al., 2014). This comes from the inefficiencies in growing cereal crops for animal feed and methane produced from livestock.

2 IT SAVES WATER

Meat production, especially the feeding of cattle, is a particularly water-intensive process. Animal agriculture uses more than 34 trillion gallons of water annually. Not eating meat will save water.

■ Around 70 percent of all freshwater used by humans goes into irrigation, and much of it is used on crops and pasture for livestock.

■ 2 lb of beef requires approximately 43,000 litres of water to produce it, which is almost 50 times more than that required to produce 2 lb vegetables (Pimentel et al., 2004).

■ Animal farming is responsible for up to 33 percent of all fresh-water consumption in the world.

■ 780 million people (1 in 10) lack access to safe water.

3 IT DOESN'T DESTROY SPECIES

No one wants to see species destroyed, but by eating meat you are unwittingly contributing to the daily loss of more than 100 species of animals, plants, and insects in the world. Huge areas of the rainforest are being cut down to graze livestock and grow crops for animal feed. By removing rainforest, habitats are also lost and so are thousands of animal, plant, and insect species (www.savetheamazon.org/rainforeststats.htm).

4 IT PROTECTS THE OCEANS

Three quarters of the world's fisheries are exploited or depleted. Overfishing depletes the oceans and damages wildlife. For every pound of fish caught, five pounds of bi-kill (other fish or sea animals) are also caught and wasted. A lot of sea bird populations are now threatened because there are not enough fish for them to survive on. There is also the problem of dolphins, whales, turtles, and other sea birds being killed when they get caught up in discarded fishing tackle and drift nets.

■ As many as 40 percent of fish caught globally each year are discarded (Goldenberg, 2014).
■ Scientists estimate as many as 650,000 whales, dolphins, and seals are also killed every year by fishing vessels.

5 IT'S A BETTER USE OF LAND

Rearing animals for meat is a very wasteful and inefficient way of producing food for people. Switching to a plant-based diet is a far more economical use of land. Growing crops to feed people rather than animals uses less land, water, and other resources, will help save land, and improve global food security. Cattle ranching is also one of the main causes of tropical rainforest destruction. Fast-shrinking rainforests are often cut down for cattle pasture or to grow crops for animal feed.

■ 30 percent of the earth's entire land surface—70 percent of all agricultural land—is used to produce animal products.
■ It takes $1/6$th of an acre to feed a vegan, 3 times as much for a vegetarian, and 18 times as much for a meat-eater.
■ Animals eat half of the wheat and 60 percent of the barley grown in the UK, and 80 percent of the world's soy beans.

IT'S GOOD FOR THE PLANET

Plant-based diets use fewer natural resources. One study from the University of Oxford estimated that changing to a more plant-based diet in line with the WHO's global dietary guidelines would cut food-related greenhouse gas emissions by more than two thirds (Springmann et. al., 2016).

■ For every 2 lb of beef produced, cattle consume 15.4 lb of grain.
■ 1.5 acres of land can produce 37,000 lb of plant-based food, whereas the same amount of land produces just 374.7 lb meat.
■ Livestock production is responsible for 70 percent of the Amazon deforestation in Latin America, where the rainforest has been cleared to create new pastures.

6 IT CAUSES LESS POLLUTION AND WASTE

Animal waste causes substantial water and air pollution, and emits nitrous oxide and methane. In the UK, intensive factory farming is one of the main causes of water pollution. Farm runoff results in high levels of nitrogen in rivers and oceans, which pollutes coastal water, kills marine life, and can result in ocean dead zones.

■ US livestock in confined feedlots generate 500 million tons of manure a year, three times the waste of the entire human population.
■ A farm of 2,500 dairy cows generates the same amount of waste as a city of 411,000 people.

7 IT'S ETHICAL

For many, choosing a vegetarian lifestyle is an ethical decision. They believe that rearing and killing animals for meat is morally wrong; that eating meat is a form of exploitation and cruelty to animals. By not eating meat, they are helping to prevent this exploitation. Vegetarians also believe that animals have rights—a right to life and to freedom, and that it is unethical to raise and kill them so that we can eat meat and fish. Whether or not animals are reared in decent conditions or treated "humanely," this does not justify raising and killing them for meat. In the end, they have their lives cut short. The truth is we don't need to eat meat to live nor to be healthy. We can obtain a perfectly healthy diet by eating other foods.

■ In the UK, over two million land animals are slaughtered daily and almost 600,000 tons of fish are killed each year.
■ Beef cattle are slaughtered when they are just 1–2 years old, considerably less than their natural lifespan of 20–25 years.
■ Sheep naturally live for 15 years but are killed when they are between 3 and 10 months old.
■ Pigs also live for 15 years but their lives are cut short when they are 3–6 months old.
■ Chickens can live for 10 years but are killed at just 6 weeks.

animals in such conditions. Most animals raised for meat don't have access to fresh air, proper exercise, or the freedom to behave naturally. They may experience pain, discomfort, fear, and frustration. Ultimately, whether they are reared on a factory or free-range farm, all animals die a violent death at the slaughterhouse when they are still very young.

■ Many beef cattle are kept indoors all year-round.
■ Most of the pigs in the UK are reared intensively in over-crowded sheds and with no outdoor access.
■ The majority of broiler chickens live in large, windowless, crowded sheds. The birds are fattened up so quickly that their legs may not be able to carry the weight of their bodies.
■ Sheep may spend most of their lives outdoors, but each year 1 in 20 die of cold, starvation, sickness, or injury. Many are transported long distances to slaughter, which is stressful.
■ Fish may be dragged along the ocean bed for long periods in giant drift nets and undergo painful decompression when hauled up from the deep. On some ships, fish are gutted alive.
■ Free-range doesn't mean cruelty free. Animals are often kept in crowded conditions with restricted access to outdoors. They are still slaughtered at an early age in the same way as intensively reared animals.

8 IT'S COMPASSIONATE TO ANIMALS

Many people choose not to eat meat because they are concerned about animal suffering. Many animals farmed for meat are kept in filthy and cramped factory farms and never experience a natural life out in the open air. They are kept in small spaces indoors so that farmers can cut costs and produce meat as quickly and cheaply as possible. Vegetarians believe it is cruel to keep

9 IT'S HEALTHIER

People living in the five regions of the world identified as having the highest concentrations of centenarians in the world (the so-called Blue Zones: Sardinia; Okinawa in Japan; Ikaria in Greece; the Nicoya peninsula of Costa Rica; and Loma Linda in Southern California) live on a mainly plant-based or semi-vegetarian diet. The Sardinians, for example, eat meat once or twice a week, and the people of Okinawa, Japan, get only 7 percent of their calories from protein—the majority of which comes from sweet potatoes.

Many leading health organizations suggest that eating less meat and more plant foods has definite nutritional and health benefits. The British Dietetic Association states that "well planned vegetarian diets can be nutritious and healthy" (BDA, 2014). This is in agreement with the position paper on vegetarian diets from the Academy of Nutrition and Dietetics (formerly the American Dietetic Association), which states that "appropriately planned vegetarian diets, including total vegetarian or vegan diets, are healthful, nutritionally adequate, and may provide health benefits in the prevention and treatment of certain diseases" (Craig et al., 2009). Indeed, hundreds of studies suggest that vegetarians have longer lives and are at lower risk of developing:

- Heart disease
- High blood pressure
- Type 2 diabetes
- Obesity
- Certain cancers

Large-scale prospective dietary surveys have found that vegetarians typically have higher intakes of fruit and vegetables, fiber, antioxidant nutrients, and phytochemicals (plant substances that have beneficial health properties) and lower intakes of saturated fat than non-vegetarians (Spencer et al., 2003; Key et al., 1999). It is possible that other lifestyle factors may also play a role—vegetarians generally weigh less, exercise more, and are less likely to smoke and drink excessive alcohol; all of which may account for some of the reduction in disease risk.

Our knowledge of the benefits of a vegetarian diet comes mainly from these large-scale cohort studies:

VEGETARIANISM IS GOOD FOR YOUR BRAIN

Vegetarian diets are associated with a lower risk of depression, according to a Spanish study of 15,000 people which found that those eating a mainly plant-based diet—including a vegetarian diet—were 25 to 30 percent less likely to be diagnosed with depression over a 10-year period (Sánchez-Villegas et al., 2015).

- The European Prospective Investigation into Cancer and Nutrition (EPIC) study, an ongoing prospective study begun in 1992, has looked at the relationship between diet, lifestyle, and cancer in approximately half a million people from 10 European countries.
- EPIC-Oxford is part of the EPIC study and looks at how diet influences the risk of cancer and other chronic diseases in a cohort (group) of 65,000 people in the UK.
- The Oxford Vegetarian Study, a prospective study of the health of 6,000 vegetarians and 5,000 non-vegetarians in the UK that began in the early 80s and followed them over 12 years.
- The Adventist Health Studies (Adventist Mortality Study, Adventist Health Study, and Adventist Health Study-2) carried out by researchers at Loma Linda University, USA, tracked the diets and lifestyles of thousands of Seventh-day Adventists in the US and Canada. Adventists have a lower risk of heart disease and other chronic diseases than other Americans due in part to their unique dietary habits. About half of them are vegetarian and, for religious reasons, they also abstain from tobacco and alcohol. This therefore presents an ideal opportunity for scientists to compare various vegetarian dietary patterns, while eliminating confounding factors, such as alcohol and smoking.

IT HELPS YOU LIVE LONGER

People who have followed a vegetarian diet for at least 17 years live nearly 4 years longer than meat-eaters, according to research at the Mayo Clinic, Arizona (Fields et al., 2016). An analysis of six prospective studies by researchers at Loma Linda University, California, USA, concluded that people who eat very little meat live longer than average (Singh et al., 2003). Those who ate this way for 20 years or more had the lowest risk of dying early. Similarly, an analysis of the three Adventist studies found that people following a vegetarian diet lived longer and had lower risks for heart disease, stroke, and certain cancers than meat-eaters (Le & Sabate, 2014). One of these studies, the Adventist Health Study-2 involving 96,000 people, found those who excluded meat had a 12 percent lower risk of death from any cause in a 6-year follow-up compared with non-vegetarians (Orlich et al., 2013).

IT'S GOOD FOR YOUR HEART

One of the major findings of the Adventist Health Studies was the low risk of heart disease among vegetarians compared with meat-eaters (Snowdon, 1988; Key et al., 1999; Orlich et al., 2013). This was echoed in the more recent EPIC-Oxford study, the largest ever carried out in the UK, which tracked the diets of 45,000 people in England and Scotland, a third of whom were

vegetarians. It found that vegetarians were 32 percent less likely to develop heart disease compared with meat and fish-eaters (Crowe et al., 2013). After 10 years, researchers found that the vegetarians were also less likely to be overweight, less likely to have type 2 diabetes, and had lower blood pressure and LDL-cholesterol levels. These health benefits may be explained by their higher intakes of fruit, vegetables, nuts, beans, and lentils, which are rich sources of soluble fiber. Soluble fiber lowers blood cholesterol levels. Also plant foods contain thousands of phytochemicals and healthy unsaturated oils that help reduce chronic low-grade inflammation—a process that is intimately involved in the development of atherosclerosis, heart attacks, strokes, and even vascular dementia.

It's not essential to be fully vegetarian to benefit from eating less meat. In a 2015 study carried out by researchers at Imperial College London as part of the EPIC project, those who consumed at least 70 percent of their food from plant sources had a 20 percent lower risk of succumbing to heart disease or stroke (Lassale et al., 2015).

CUTS CANCER RISK

Many studies have shown that populations that eat less meat tend to have less cancer, particularly bowel, breast, and prostate cancers. The EPIC-Oxford study found that vegetarians are less likely to develop cancer than meat-eaters, partly due to the absence of meat and partly to the increased intake of fruit, vegetables, and fiber (Key et al., 2009).

Bowel cancer is more common among people who eat the most red meat and processed meat. Processed meat refers to meat that has been smoked, cured, or had salt or chemical preservatives added, and includes ham, bacon, some sausages, beef jerky, salami, chorizo, pepperoni, and frankfurters. According to the 2007 expert report by the World Cancer Research Fund (WCRF) and the American Institute of Cancer Research (AICR), eating even a small amount of processed meat on a regular basis greatly increases bowel cancer risk (WCRF/AICR, 2007). It also found that eating more than 1 lb of red meat per week increases the risk. Another report by the researchers at the WCRF in 2011 confirmed this risk (Chan et al., 2011). For this reason, both the WCRF and the National Health Service (NHS) recommend eating no more than 1 lb of meat a week (or 70 g a

day), and as little processed meat as possible.

The strongest evidence comes from a report by the World Health Organisation's International Agency for Research on Cancer (WHO/IARC) which ruled that processed meat "definitely" causes cancer and that red meat "probably" causes cancer (Bouvard et al., 2015). It put processed meat in the same class of cancer risk as cigarettes, asbestos, and alcohol (Group I carcinogens), which means that the experts are very confident that it causes cancer (although they do not say how many cancers it causes). The report concluded that 1.7 ounces of processed meat a day is enough to significantly increase bowel cancer risk by 18 percent.

The EPIC study found that consuming processed meat increased the risk of dying from both heart disease and cancer (Rohrmann et al., 2013). These results were based on an analysis of almost half a million people aged between 35 and 69. Researchers also found that bowel cancer was 30 percent more common among people who ate 5.6 ounces of red and processed meat day, compared with those who ate less than 0.7 ounces (Norat et al., 2005). An analysis of 29 studies concluded that a high consumption of red meat increases risk by 28 percent and a high consumption of processed meat increases risk by 20 percent (Larsson & Wolk, 2006).

IT CAN HELP LOWER YOUR BLOOD PRESSURE

Fruit, vegetables, beans, lentils, whole grains, nuts, and seeds are all packed with potassium, which helps lower blood pressure and improve heart health. The EPIC-Oxford study found that vegetarians had lower blood pressure and less hypertension than meat-eaters, although this may be partly explained by their lower body weight (high blood pressure is associated with obesity) (Appleby et al., 2002). In the Adventist Health Study-2, vegetarians were 55 percent less likely to develop hypertension than meat-eaters (Pettersen et al., 2012; Le and Sabate, 2014).

IT LOWERS CHOLESTEROL

The Oxford Vegetarian Study, involving 11,000 people, found that vegetarians had lower levels of total and low-density lipoprotein (LDL) cholesterol than meat-eaters (Appleby et al., 1999). This is thought to be due to the unique combination of fiber, vitamins, and phytochemicals found in plants. According to a 2005 study, adding more nuts, seeds, whole grains, and fruit and vegetables to your diet is a more effective way to lower harmful LDL blood cholesterol and heart disease risk than cutting fat or saturated fat (Gardner et al., 2005).

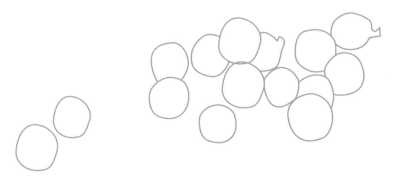

IT WILL HELP YOU LOSE WEIGHT

Generally, vegetarians weigh less and have a lower Body Mass Index (BMI) than meat-eaters (Appleby & Key, 2015, Spencer et al., 2003). This is partly due to healthier lifestyles but also due to the fact that plant-based foods contain significantly fewer calories than meat—eating more of them means you're less hungry and more satisfied after eating. An analysis of 12 studies involving 1150 people on different weight loss plans found that dieters who ate a vegetarian or vegan diet lost more weight than those who ate meat over 18 weeks (Huang et al., 2016). Those who followed a vegetarian weight-loss diet lost roughly 4 lb more on average than those whose meals included meat. Their success may be explained by the fact that vegetarian diets are rich in fruit, vegetables, and whole grains, which are high in fiber. They take longer to digest and keep you feeling fuller longer. The researchers also found that people who gave up meat to lose weight were more likely to still be following their healthy eating plan one year later than those who consumed meat.

Beans, lentils, chickpeas, vegetables, nuts, and whole grains are not only filling but they may also help people lose weight by acting on gut microbes (bacteria that live in your gut) too. Fiber and polyphenols (antioxidant plant compounds) found in these foods encourage healthy gut bacteria to grow. Researchers have discovered that the more diverse your gut microbes, the more likely you are to be healthy and lean (Spector, 2015).

IT REDUCES YOUR RISK OF TYPE 2 DIABETES

In the Adventist-2 Study, the risk of type 2 diabetes was 25 to 49 percent lower in vegetarians than meat-eaters. The more meat people ate, the higher the risk (Tonstad et al., 2009). This remained true even after factors such as physical activity and BMI were controlled for. This may be explained partly by the high fiber content of vegetarian diets—which helps increase satiety (and thus reduce overeating), control blood sugar levels, and avoid blood sugar swings after meals—and partly by the absence of meat. A previous study of 37,000 women by researchers at the Brigham and Women's Hospital (affiliate of Harvard Medical School) in the US found that type 2 diabetes was more common in those who ate the most red meat and processed meat (Song et al., 2004).

VEGETARIAN MYTHS

There are many myths surrounding vegetarian diets. Here are four:

MYTH 1 VEGETARIANS DON'T GET ENOUGH PROTEIN

This is the most common myth and unfortunately it is the easiest to buy into because our society associates protein almost exclusively with meat. Most people therefore believe that meat is essential for health. However, in this country, protein deficiency is not a problem. The average person's intake is around 2.6 ounces per day, which is 40 to 70 percent more than the guideline daily amount of 1.5–1.9 ounces. The thing that people fail to realize is that many foods other than meat are an excellent source of protein.

Almost all foods contain some protein so it's not difficult to get enough protein from vegetarian sources—even if you're a heavyweight bodybuilder. Aim to get around 0.7 ounces after a workout and also at each mealtime. Opt for milk (dairy and non-dairy), yogurt, cheese, beans, lentils, soy foods, nuts, seeds, and grains. Dairy products are especially valuable to vegetarians as they provide high quality proteins containing all essential amino acids, as well as high levels of leucine, which triggers muscle protein manufacture (page 27). But with a bit of planning, it is easy to supply the body with more than enough quality protein to build and maintain muscle on a vegetarian diet. As a bonus you will also supply the body with plenty of vitamins, minerals, and other compounds such as phytochemicals and fiber that you will not find in meat.

MYTH 2 A VEGETARIAN DIET WILL LACK IRON

Iron deficiency is more likely to occur as a result of inadequate absorption or excessive loss through menstruation rather than a lack of consumption; so meat-eaters are just as susceptible to iron deficiency as vegetarians.

Many people believe that meat is the only real source of iron, but the truth is that iron is found in a wide variety of plant foods, including beans, lentils, leafy green vegetables, nuts, and seeds. Although iron is not as readily absorbed from plants, the body adapts by absorbing a higher percentage from the food we eat. In other words, it's not about how much iron you consume but how well you absorb it.

Eating food rich in vitamin C (e.g. fruit or vegetables) at the same time as iron-rich foods greatly improves iron absorption. Citric acid (found naturally in fruit and vegetables) also promotes iron absorption.

If you eat a varied diet that includes a balance of grains, legumes (dried seeds such as chickpeas and lentils), nuts, seeds, fruit, and vegetables, you are no more at risk of iron deficiency than a meat-eater.

MYTH 3 YOU'LL HAVE LESS ENERGY

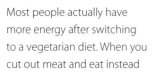

Most people actually have more energy after switching to a vegetarian diet. When you cut out meat and eat instead more beans, lentils, nuts, fruit, and vegetables, you'll automatically be getting more vitamins, minerals, and phytochemicals, which boosts immunity. If your energy levels do drop, you probably aren't matching your calories to your training, or you may not be getting the right balance of nutrients. For example, not getting enough

protein or carbohydrates means slower recovery after exercise and your muscles cannot repair themselves efficiently. Try adding more beans, lentils, dairy, grains, fruit, and nuts to your diet.

MYTH 4 VEGETARIAN DIETS LEAVE YOU HUNGRY

If you're hungry on a vegetarian diet, then you're doing something wrong—namely, not getting enough fiber. Plant-based foods, such as beans, lentils, whole grains, fruit, vegetables, nuts, and seeds, are full of fiber, which literally keeps you full for longer and stabilizes blood sugar levels to prevent cravings for unhealthy foods soon after eating. It also helps to satisfy your hunger by slowing down the rate that foods pass through your digestive system.

GOING VEGETARIAN—THE FIRST STEPS

Now you've read this far, hopefully you are convinced that a vegetarian diet is healthier, less damaging to the environment, kinder to animals, and can help you become an awesome athlete. If you're ready to give up meat, then here are some top tips:

■ You don't have to go vegetarian overnight. You can do it gradually. Try eating less meat over a few weeks, going vegetarian one day a week, then substituting more vegetarian meals for meat in both your weekday and weekend routines.

■ Try experimenting with different fresh foods and recipes to see what you like. Going vegetarian can open your eyes to a whole new world of ingredients, cooking styles, and cuisines.

■ Don't simply substitute fake meats or ready-prepared convenience foods such as veggie burgers, sausages, pizzas, and pies for meat. They are loaded with salt and low in vitamins, minerals, and fiber. Fresh and wholesome foods are a healthier way to fuel your body for exercise. The recipes in Part 2 will give you plenty of new ideas and inspiration!

■ Try adapting your favorite meals into vegetarian versions. Stir-fries, stews, curries, shepherd's pie, chili, and burgers can all be done as vegetarian meals using beans, lentils, or tofu instead of meat.

■ Try one new recipe a week. Don't worry if you're not an experienced cook—Part 2 contains lots of simple recipes that require minimal skill or cooking experience. Once you start cooking and adapting your own vegetarian meals, you'll realize there's a whole new exciting world of food out there just waiting to be discovered.

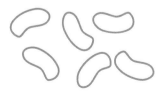

Butternut squash and pea risotto, page 134

CHAPTER 2

MAXIMIZING YOUR PERFORMANCE WITHOUT MEAT

It's a popular misconception that a vegetarian diet cannot support high-level athletic performance. Naysayers maintain that, however fit and healthy you are, you'd be fitter, healthier, faster, and all-round "better" with meat in your diet. Nothing could be further from the truth—there are plenty of examples of world-class athletes and Olympic champions who don't eat meat. Here are just a few:

Lizzie Armitstead (world track and road race cycling champion)

Brendan Brazier (professional Ironman triathlete)

Michaela Copenhaver (US national rower)

Meagan Duhamel (pairs figure skating world champion)

Prince Fielder (MLB player)

Vlad Ixel (ultra-marathon trail runner and record holder)

Scott Jurek (world class ultra-marathoner and record holder)

Jack Lindquist (professional track-racing cyclist)

Heather Mills (skeleton bobsleigh and speed skating world record holder)

Ed Moses (Olympic 400m hurdles gold medalist)

Martina Navratilova (nine-time Wimbledon tennis champion)

Pat Reeves (British masters powerlifting champion)

Dave Scott (Ironman world champion)

Kevin Selker (US national track cycling champion)

Madi Serpico (professional triathlete)

Peter Siddle (fast bowler for Australian Cricket team)

Billy Simmonds (bodybuilder and winner of Mr Natural Universe)

David Smith (paralympic and world championship cycling gold medalist)

Mike Tyson (world heavyweight boxing champion)

Kenneth G Williams (bodybuilder and winner of World Natural Bodybuilding Championships)

Venus Williams (champion tennis player and four-time Olympic gold medalist)

East African distance runners, who are among the best in the world, eat very little meat. They follow a traditional plant-based diet with lots of fresh, unprocessed foods and are testament to the benefits of a vegetarian diet.

The reality is that many non-vegetarians can't imagine a meal without meat on the plate. It is hard for them to understand why anyone would want to avoid meat and cannot fathom how anyone can stay fueled and perform well without meat protein. They think that sport and vegetarian diets just don't mix. I've even heard meat-eaters urge vegetarians to add meat back into their diet in order to improve their performance. However, there's no scientific evidence to support these views. The truth is you can get all the nutrients you need to support an intense training program without eating meat.

In 2009, the American Dietetic Association (ADA), American College of Sports Medicine (ACSM), and Dietitians of Canada (DC) published a position statement on nutrition athletic performance and concluded that "well-planned vegetarian diets appear to effectively support parameters that influence athletic performance" (ADA, 2009). This view is backed by the Australian Institute for Sport (AIS) who state that "vegetarian eating can support optimal sports performance." In other words, meat and fish are not essential for maximum performance.

In planning a vegetarian diet, it is essential to make sure it contains all the necessary nutrients you need for health and training. When healthy balanced choices are made, a vegetarian diet can easily meet the nutritional needs for any sport or lifestyle.

Provided you're careful to include a wide variety of plant foods then a vegetarian diet can fuel performance just as well as a meat-based diet. The key is knowing which foods to eat in place of meat and knowing how to incorporate them into your meals. If you're new to vegetarian eating, then this may require some initial changes to the way you shop, prepare, and cook food. But the good news is that once you've got the hang of the basic rules, then it's very easy to put together a balanced diet without meat. Whether you already follow a vegetarian diet or you're just interested in eating less meat, this chapter will explain how you can ensure you get all the right nutrients and avoid the most common pitfalls of a vegetarian diet. It focuses on the main nutrients that vegetarians and vegans often fall short on and gives practical tips on getting your daily quota.

CAN VEGETARIAN ATHLETES PERFORM AS WELL IN SPORT AS PEOPLE WHO EAT MEAT?

A 2015 analysis by Australian researchers of eight previous studies that compared the performance of athletes eating a vegetarian diet with those whose diets included meat concluded that well-planned and varied vegetarian diets neither hinder nor improve athletic performance (Craddock et al., 2015). This is in agreement with the findings of a previous review of studies by the University of British Columbia, Canada, which suggested that vegetarian diets can provide more than enough protein to support athletic training and performance (Barr & Rideout, 2004).

Several studies have measured physical fitness, limb circumference, and strength in vegetarian and non-vegetarian athletes and found no differences in any of these parameters (Nieman, 1999; Hanne et al., 1986). In other words, vegetarians were not disadvantaged in terms of their performance, fitness, or strength.

In one study, researchers asked runners to follow either a vegetarian or non-vegetarian diet for two weeks. They found no difference in running performance between the two groups, suggesting that giving up meat had no detrimental effect on short-term performance (Williams, 1985).

Among female athletes consuming a semi-vegetarian diet (less than 3.5 ounces red meat per week), there was no difference in their aerobic fitness compared with meat-eaters (Snyder, 1989).

Danish researchers tested athletes after consuming either a vegetarian or non-vegetarian diet for six weeks alternately (Richter et al., 1991). The carbohydrate content of each diet was kept the same (57 percent energy). Whichever diet they ate, the athletes experienced no change in aerobic capacity, endurance, muscle glycogen concentration, or strength.

In one study, ultra-runners completed a 621-mile race over a 20-day period after consuming either a vegetarian or non-vegetarian diet containing similar amounts of carbohydrate (60 percent energy) (Eisinger, 1994). There was no difference in performance between the two groups. In a 2002 study, athletes who followed a vegetarian diet for 12 weeks of resistance training achieved the same strength and muscle size gains as those following a non-vegetarian diet containing exactly the same amount of protein (Haub et al., 2002). In other words, when it comes to building muscle, it doesn't matter where you get your protein from, provided you're getting enough of it. Together, these studies suggest that vegetarians can perform just as well as non-vegetarians and that a well-planned vegetarian diet does not hinder athletic performance.

CAN A VEGETARIAN DIET MAKE YOU A BETTER ATHLETE?

In his autobiographical book, *Eat & Run*, Scott Jurek, a vegan ultra-runner, explains that he turned vegetarian then vegan in order to run faster, not for ethics or health. He ran the Minnesota Voyageur 50-mile race twice before he won. The only difference he identified on that third occasion was his diet.

"I won the Voyageur on my third try, eating more plants and less meat. I didn't run harder. I had been right: I couldn't run harder. But I had learned something important. I could run smarter. I could eat smarter."

On the other hand, he admits that his previous diet had been poor, so any conscious change would have been good, whether vegan or not. To date, no studies have examined whether a vegetarian diet will *improve* athletic performance, so we don't know with certainty the true benefits of a vegetarian diet on exercise performance. Studies have either controlled for the inherent differences seen between vegetarian diets and non-vegetarian diets (for example, matching carbohydrate or protein), or have used populations that are not representative of well-trained athletes.

In theory, if a vegetarian diet met or exceeded recommendations for energy (calories), protein, carbohydrate, and other nutrients, then it would match the ideal or recommended diet for training and recovery. As vegetarians generally consume more fiber and phytonutrients, further research is required to determine the possible training and competition benefits of following such a diet.

WHAT ARE THE PITFALLS OF A VEGETARIAN DIET?

While there's no doubt that a well-planned vegetarian diet can support a hard training program, it is important to understand that simply taking meat off your plate is not enough to guarantee health. Unfortunately, some people assume that simply eliminating meat from their diet will automatically make them healthier. Many have tried this approach to vegetarianism unsuccessfully and returned to their old ways, blaming the diet for leaving them feeling run down, ill, and tired.

If one food type is taken out of your diet and not replaced with healthy alternatives, an imbalance can occur which can lead to a variety of problems. A bowl of pasta with tomato sauce contains no meat but it hardly classifies as a balanced meal.

If you don't substitute the right types of foods, you will almost certainly miss out on key nutrients. The most common pitfalls are a lack of protein, iron, omega-3 fats, and vitamin D. Vegans may also fall short on vitamin B_{12} and calcium. Deficiencies of these nutrients will affect your performance and health, and increase your risk of illness, fatigue, and injury. The good news is that by eating alternative foods, you can easily obtain all nutrients you need for peak health and performance.

GETTING A BALANCED AND NUTRITIOUS DIET

PROTEIN

Although meat may be a concentrated source of protein, you can easily obtain sufficient protein from other foods. Dairy foods, beans, lentils, tofu, and eggs, for example, are all excellent sources of protein so it's not difficult to get your daily quota.

One of the biggest fallacies about vegetarian diets is that they can't provide enough protein to build muscle. Skeptics like to point out that vegetarians eat less protein than meat-eaters. So what? This doesn't mean that vegetarians are lacking in protein or that you can't build muscle or perform to your potential in sport. In fact, studies show that well-planned vegetarian diets can easily meet the protein needs of athletes (Venderley & Campbell, 2006). According to the Academy of Nutrition and Dietetics "vegetarian diets that meet energy needs and contain a variety of plant-based protein foods, such

FIVE TO FOCUS ON

1 DAIRY PRODUCTS such as milk, yogurt, cheese
2 EGGS
3 BEANS AND LENTILS
4 SOY PRODUCTS such as tofu
5 NUTS AND SEEDS

as soy products, other legumes, grains, nuts, and seeds, can provide adequate protein without the use of special foods or supplements"(Craig & Mangels., 2009).

When we talk about protein we are really talking about amino acids. These are the building blocks of proteins that are combined in many different ways to make hundreds of different proteins. They each have specific roles in metabolism and muscle building and are used for repairing and rebuilding the muscle fibers that you have damaged during your workout. Eight cannot be created in the body and are therefore called "essential amino acids." These must be provided by the diet.

It is the amount of these essential amino acids in foods that determine how useful the protein is to the body. People often talk about which protein is "better" for you, but what they really mean is which protein has a profile of essential amino acids most closely matched to body proteins. Foods containing high levels of all of the essential amino acids are often regarded as "high-quality" proteins. For vegetarians, these include dairy products, eggs, and soy. On the other hand, plant sources such as beans, lentils, nuts, seeds, and grains are lacking in one or more essential amino acid so are not as "complete" or useful on their own. If you ate, say, lentils, and nothing else, you may not get enough of the amino acid methionine. As an athlete, this would limit your muscle growth.

The main argument against vegetarian diets is that the protein is inferior or less bioavailable (less available to the body). However, the key to a healthy vegetarian diet is to eat a variety of foods containing protein. This means that the shortfall of amino acids in one food (e.g. methionine in lentils) is complemented by the higher amounts found in another (e.g. in rice). For example, rice with lentils would provide more than enough methionine along with all the other essential amino acids. This is called "protein complementation." Combining rice with lentils, for example, gives a better complement of amino acids needed to make new body proteins than eating either foods on their own. You can achieve protein complementation by combining foods from two or more of the following categories:

1. **LEGUMES:** beans, lentils, peas
2. **GRAINS:** bread, pasta, rice, oats, breakfast cereals, quinoa
3. **NUTS AND SEEDS:** peanuts, cashews, almonds, sunflower seeds, sesame seeds, pumpkin seeds
4. **DAIRY PRODUCTS:** milk, cheese, yogurt, eggs
5. **SOY PRODUCTS:** milk, yogurt, tofu, soy beans, edamame beans

It is not necessary to always combine proteins within a single meal. Our bodies pool the amino acids we need as we eat them over a 24-hour period and we use them as needed (Young & Pellett, 1994). This means you don't have to worry about combining proteins at every meal and snack, provided you consume enough protein throughout the day and from a wide variety of sources. However, many food combinations happen naturally in certain meals, including in the following examples:

- Vegetarian chili (legumes) with rice (grain)
- Dhal (legumes) with chapati (grain)
- Tofu (soy) stir-fry with noodles (grain)
- Toast (grain) with peanut butter (nuts)

Vegetarians who consume dairy and eggs obviously have more choice. A meal that includes milk, cheese, yogurt, or eggs will contain sufficient essential amino acids. Combining them with another protein source will augment the meal's overall protein value. Vegans, however, need to ensure they eat sufficient amounts of plant proteins, such as beans, lentils, nuts, tofu, and seeds.

*Tofu and vegetable
stir-fry, page 143*

HOW MUCH DO YOU NEED?

The protein needs of athletes are higher than those of the general population. This is due to exercise-induced muscle breakdown and the resultant need to repair damaged muscle cells after exercise (Rodriquez et al., 2009; Phillips et al, 2007; Campbell et al., 2007). Additional protein is also needed to support gains in muscle mass.

For non-athletes the recommended daily allowance (RDA) for protein is 0.8 grams per kilogram of body weight per day. For athletes, the protein recommendation is between 1.2 and 1.8 g protein per kilogram of body weight per day, depending on the type, intensity, and duration of training; with intakes at the higher end of this range (approximately 1.6 to 1.8 g/kg) recommended for strength and power athletes (Phillips & Van Loon, 2011) and intakes at the lower end of the range (approximately 1.2 to 1.4 g/kg) for endurance athletes. For a 154 lb person, this translates to between 112 and 126 g daily for strength training and 84 to 98 g daily for endurance training. This amount can easily be obtained from a vegetarian diet.

You can achieve this by eating a wide variety of nuts, seeds, beans, lentils, dairy foods, soy products (tofu, tempeh), cereals (oats, pasta, rice, millet and other grains), bread, and quinoa, as well as eggs. Aim for around 20 g per meal, including post-training (see page 46). Studies by researchers at McMaster University have shown this to be the optimal amount to trigger muscle growth and recovery (Moore et al., 2009; Moore et al., 2012). Contrary to popular belief, this isn't hard to achieve in a vegetarian diet. The key is to include a portion of beans, chickpeas, or lentils plus a portion of grains or nuts. All the breakfast and main meal recipes in Part 2 provide approximately 20 g protein per serving.

The table opposite gives you the protein content of various vegetarian options within different food groups.

Red lentil and vegetable soup, page 81

FOOD PROVIDING 20 G PROTEIN

- 3 eggs
- 20 ounces milk (or flavored milk)
- 1 ounce whey protein powder
- 3 ounces Cheddar cheese
- 16 ounces plain yogurt
- 8 ounces strained Greek yogurt
- 1 can (14 ounces) chickpeas or beans (equivalent to 8 ounces drained weight)
- 7 ounces nuts
- 9.5 ounces tofu

HOW MUCH PROTEIN?

FOOD	AMOUNT OF PROTEIN
DAIRY PRODUCTS	
1 slice (1 oz) Cheddar cheese	6 g
1 slice (1 oz) Mozzarella	5 g
2 tbsp (3.5 oz) cottage cheese	12 g
2 eggs	12 g
1 cup (approx. 8 oz) milk (all types)	8 g
1 small pot (approx. 4 oz) plain yogurt	6 g
3 tbsp (approx. 5 oz) low-fat plain Greek yogurt	11 g
3 tbsp (approx. 5 oz) strained low-fat plain Greek yogurt	15 g
BEANS AND LENTILS	
4 heaped tbsp (7 oz) edamame beans	22 g
3.5 oz tofu	13 g
4 heaped tbsp (7 oz) cooked beans (2.5 oz dry weight)	18 g
4 heaped tbsp (7 oz) cooked lentils (2.5 oz dry weight)	18 g
NUTS AND SEEDS	
1 small handful (1 oz) pumpkin seeds	7 g
1 small handful (1 oz) almonds	6 g
1 small handful (1 oz) peanuts	7 g
1 small handful (1 oz) cashews	5 g
1 tablespoon (1 oz) peanut butter	7 g
GRAINS AND "PSEUDOGRAINS"	
4 tbsp (2 oz) oats (dry weight)	7 g
5 heaped tbsp (9 oz) cooked quinoa (2.5 oz dry weight)	11 g
5 heaped tbsp (9 oz) cooked pasta (2.5 oz dry weight)	10 g
5 heaped tbsp (9 oz) cooked noodles (2.5 oz dry weight)	6 g
5 heaped tbsp (9 oz) cooked brown rice (2.5 oz dry weight)	7 g
1 slice wholegrain bread (1.4 oz)	4 g
1 wholegrain pita (2 oz)	6 g
VEGETABLES	
3 sprigs (3.5 oz) broccoli	4 g
1 potato	3 g
3 tbsp (3.5 oz) spinach	2 g

SHOULD VEGETARIAN ATHLETES TAKE SUPPLEMENTS?

If you already get enough protein from food, then there's little point in taking supplements. They won't improve your performance, build bigger muscles, or hasten recovery. However, if you find it difficult to meet your protein quota from food alone, or if you follow a vegan diet, then protein supplements are a good alternative. They are convenient and can make it easier to obtain your daily protein. Many athletes use them immediately after exercise—studies show that consuming 20 g of protein promotes muscle recovery (Moore et al., 2009), which you can get from 1 scoop of whey protein powder. However, you can also get this amount from 2 cups of milk. Studies have shown that drinking milk after exercise is just as effective as whey protein supplements (Cockburn et al., 2012). If you use almond or rice milk, then bear in mind these are much lower in protein than ordinary (dairy) milk or soy milk. Try adding a scoop of vegan protein powder to a shake or smoothie to boost your protein intake. These contain protein from peas, brown rice, soy, or hemp or a mixture of these.

RECIPES PROVIDING 20 G PROTEIN

- Black bean and vegetable curry with almonds, below (page 103)
- Dhal with butternut squash and spinach (page 108)
- Sweet potato and chickpea curry with cashews (page 109)
- Puy lentil lasagna (page 113)
- Lentil, quinoa, and bean bake (page 116)
- Mixed bean and lentil hotpot with fresh cilantro (page 117)
- Red lentil shepherd's pie (page 128)
- Quinoa lentil bolognese (page 129)

CREATINE

CAN VEGETARIANS GAIN MORE BENEFITS FROM CREATINE SUPPLEMENTS THAN MEAT-EATERS?

As vegetarians have lower creatine levels in their muscles than meat-eaters (creatine is found only in meat and fish), they stand to benefit the most from supplementation. Creatine supplements increase muscle levels of phosphocreatine, an energy-rich compound made from creatine and phosphorus that fuels muscles during high intensity exercise, such as sprinting or lifting weights. In one study, vegetarian athletes who took creatine supplements for eight weeks while following a resistance training program experienced a greater increase in phosphocreatine, muscle mass, and exercise performance than those who took a placebo, which suggests that vegetarians are more responsive to creatine (Burke et al., 2003). Overall, creatine helps promote muscle growth, increases muscle mass, improves strength and power, improves the ability to perform multiple bouts of high-intensity exercise, improves performance during high-intensity exercise, and improves recovery after endurance exercise (Cooper et al., 2012). The quickest way of increasing your creatine stores is to "load" with 0.3 g/kg of body weight for 5 to 7 days. That's 20 g/day for a 154 lb person. Take this amount in four equally divided doses through the day, e.g. 4 x 5 g. Alternatively, you can "load" with a smaller dose of 2–3 g/day for 3 to 4 weeks. Following the loading phase you can switch to a maintenance dose of 0.03 g/kg of body weight a day, or 2 g/day for a 154 lb person.

IRON

Iron is an essential nutrient which means your body cannot make it and it must be provided by your diet. It is needed for:

■ Making hemoglobin, the oxygen-carrying protein in red blood cells.
■ Making myoglobin, the protein that carries and stores oxygen in your muscle cells.
■ Aerobic energy production (the "electron transport system" that controls the release of energy from cells).
■ A healthy immune system.

All athletes, whether vegetarian or not, are at greater risk of developing iron deficiency compared with non-athletes. That's because aerobic training increases red blood cell manufacture, which in turn increases iron needs. At the same time, iron can be lost from the body via sweat, through gastrointestinal bleeding (which sometimes occurs during very strenuous exercise), and through foot-strike hemolysis (destruction of red blood cells caused by repeated pounding of the feet on hard surfaces). Women in general are more susceptible than men to iron deficiency due to menstruation.

It is estimated that 30 percent of female athletes, although not anemic, have iron deficiency. This is termed "non-anemic iron deficiency," or "latent iron deficiency." Iron deficiency can

Overnight oats with blueberries, page 59

reduce the amount of oxygen delivered to the muscles during exercise, as well as the amount of energy that can be generated in muscle cells. It reduces your maximal oxygen consumption (VO_2 max), your endurance capacity, and your performance. So getting enough iron and avoiding deficiency is essential. The American College of Sports Medicine states that iron deficiency can have negative effects on exercise performance as well as bone health (Rodriguez et al., 2009).

Theoretically, vegetarians are at even greater risk of iron deficiency because they don't eat meat and fish. These foods contain "heme iron," which the body can absorb more readily

FIVE TO FOCUS ON

1 WHOLE GRAINS AND "PSEUDOGRAINS": oats, brown rice, bulgur wheat, wholegrain pasta, couscous, bread, barley, and the pseudograin, quinoa (which is technically a seed, see page 105), and fortified breakfast cereals

2 NUTS AND SEEDS: cashews, almonds, walnuts, pecans, and peanuts; pumpkin, sesame and sunflower seeds

3 LEGUMES: BEANS, LENTILS, AND TOFU
4 GREEN LEAFY VEGETABLES, e.g. broccoli, cabbage, Cavolo Nero (also called Tuscan kale or dinosaur kale), chard, kale, watercress, and spinach
5 DRIED FRUIT: apricots, figs, and prunes

than "non-heme iron" from plants (such as wholegrain cereals, egg yolks, beans, lentils, green leafy vegetables, dried apricots, nuts, and seeds). Although the body only absorbs about 10 percent of iron from our food, it absorbs considerably less (typically 3 times less) from plant foods compared with meat.

But don't fret! There is evidence that the body adapts over time by increasing the percentage of iron it absorbs from food. So, if your diet contains only small amounts of non-heme iron, a higher percentage of it will be absorbed. Also, the body adjusts its absorption according to its iron needs. For example, if your iron stores dip, the body absorbs more to replenish them; similarly when iron stores are "full" then the body absorbs less.

Studies suggest that although vegetarians have slightly lower stores of iron than non-vegetarians, iron-deficiency anemia is no more common in vegetarians than meat-eaters (Ball & Bartlett, 1999; Alexander et al., 1998; Janelle & Barr, 1995). According to a review of studies by the Academy of Nutrition and Dietetics, iron and hemoglobin levels are still well within the normal range (Craig et al., 2009). Researchers have found that blood levels of hemoglobin and running performance are very similar between non-vegetarian and vegetarian female runners (Snyder, 1989;

Seiler, 1989). While these statistics may be reassuring, you should not be complacent about iron—you still need to make sure you consume enough!

SYMPTOMS OF DEFICIENCY

The symptoms of iron deficiency are all associated with decreased oxygen supply to the tissues. These include tiredness, chronic fatigue, pallor, headaches, light-headedness, above-normal breathlessness during exercise, and palpitations, frequent injuries, loss of endurance and power, loss of appetite, and loss of interest in training. Iron also plays an important role in the immune system, so people with low iron levels are more susceptible to infections.

The early symptoms of iron deficiency, such as tiredness and fatigue, are easy to miss and it's not until stores become significantly depleted that symptoms become more noticeable. When this happens, the body makes smaller red blood cells with less hemoglobin. This impairs your body's ability to carry oxygen around the body and will certainly affect your performance. If you are in doubt about your iron intake or you have any of the iron deficiency symptoms listed

THE 3 STAGES OF IRON DEFICIENCY

1 **Storage iron depletion**—when serum ferritin levels drop below 18 nanograms per milliliter (ng/ml)
2 **Early functional deficiency**—when red blood cell formation starts to become impaired but is enough to cause anemia
3 **Iron deficiency anemia**—when hemoglobin levels fall below 13 g/100 ml in men and below 12 g/100 ml in women; ferritin levels below 12 ng/ml

above, talk to your doctor. A simple blood test can determine your iron status.

HOW MUCH DO YOU NEED?

The US recommended intake is 8 mg/day for men; 18 mg/day for women aged 19 to 50; and 8 mg/day for women over 50. There is no official recommendation for athletes or for vegetarians but the requirement for iron is thought to be 30–70 percent higher (Rodriguez et al., 2009). The table on page 34 shows the iron content of popular vegetarian foods.

HOW TO BOOST IRON ABSORPTION

Fortunately, there are four ways to increase the absorption of non-heme iron from your food:

1   ALWAYS EAT VITAMIN C-RICH FOODS, such as red peppers, broccoli, spinach, tomatoes, oranges, berries (strawberries, raspberries, blueberries, blackberries), or kiwi fruit at the same time as iron-rich foods—this greatly improves iron absorption. For example, stir a handful of spinach into a dhal or lentil stew, add broccoli to a tofu stir-fry, add tomatoes and peppers to a bean hot pot, or add a handful of berries to your porridge or muesli.

2   INCLUDE FRUIT AND VEGETABLES IN EVERY MEAL—the citric acid found naturally in fruit and vegetables also promotes iron absorption. All the recipes in this book include vegetables, which will boost iron absorption from the meal. If you have a wholegrain cheese sandwich, for example, then eat some fresh fruit at the same time. If you're having beans on wholegrain toast (both good iron sources), add a leafy salad or a couple of mandarin oranges.

3   AVOID DRINKING COFFEE OR TEA WITH YOUR MEAL—they contain tannins which reduce iron absorption. Wait at least an hour after your meal before having a cup.

4   AVOID BRAN-ENRICHED BREAKFAST CEREALS, such as bran flakes and All-Bran—bran contains high levels of phytates, which inhibit the absorption of iron.

SHOULD VEGETARIAN ATHLETES TAKE SUPPLEMENTS?

The 2009 consensus statement from the American Dietary Association and American College of Sports Medicine states that all athletes—either vegetarian or meat-eating—should be periodically screened for iron status (Rodriguez et al., 2009).

If iron deficiency is diagnosed, your doctor will recommend supplements. These may be taken in liquid or pill form. The usual recommended dose is 60–100 mg iron per day taken in the form of iron sulphate for three months, although doses depend on gender, weight, and iron level.

However, if you are not deficient then you shouldn't take supplements—they won't benefit your performance and may do more harm than good. Supplements containing more than 50–60 mg of iron may cause constipation and stomach discomfort.

HOW IS IRON DEFICIENCY DIAGNOSED?

Iron deficiency in athletes is usually diagnosed by measuring ferritin (a protein in the blood that stores iron), which gives a fairly accurate indication of the body's iron stores. Your doctor may also measure levels of iron, hemoglobin (the iron-containing protein in red blood cells that carries oxygen around the body), and hematocrit (the volume percentage of red blood cells in the blood). The average person will have normal ferritin levels of between 12 to 300 nanograms per milliliter (ng/ml) for men and 12 to 150 ng/ml for women. Athletes may begin to have iron deficiency symptoms (fatigue, decreased performance, etc.) when the ferritin falls below 30 ng/ml. Iron deficiency anemia is defined as having hemoglobin levels below 13 g/100 ml in men and below 12 g/100 ml in women. Since low iron stores take 3 to 6 months to recover, early diagnosis can help to avoid training and performance problems.

HOW MUCH IRON?

FOOD	AMOUNT OF IRON
5 heaped tbsp (9 oz) cooked quinoa (2.5 oz dry weight)	5.9 mg
4 heaped tbsp (9 oz) cooked beans (2.5 oz dry weight)	5.0 mg
4 heaped tbsp (9 oz) cooked lentils (2.5 oz dry weight)	4.8 mg
4 heaped tbsp (9 oz) cooked chick peas beans (2.5 oz dry weight)	4.2 mg
4 ready-to-eat dried figs (3.5 oz)	3.9 mg
3.5 oz tofu	3.5 mg
5 heaped tbsp (9 oz) cooked wholegrain pasta (2.5 oz dry weight)	3.5 mg
8 ready-to-eat dried apricots (3.5 oz)	3.4 mg
Baked beans (½ can; 7 oz)	2.8 mg
1 tbsp (1 oz) tahini	2.7 mg
1 small handful (1 oz) pumpkin seeds	2.5 mg
3 tbsp (3.5 oz) spinach	2.1 mg
1.7 oz oats	2.0 mg
2 slices wholegrain bread (2.8 oz)	1.9 mg
2 oz muesli	1.8 mg
3 tbsp (3.5 oz) broccoli	1.7 mg
2 eggs	1.7 mg
3 tbsp (3.5 oz) kale	1.7 mg
1 small handful (1 oz) cashews	1.6 mg
5 heaped tbsp (9 oz) cooked brown rice (2.5 oz dry weight)	1.3 mg
3 tbsp (3.5 oz) Savoy cabbage	1.1 mg

THE DIFFERENCE BETWEEN ANEMIA
AND SPORTS ANEMIA

It can sometimes be difficult to assess iron status from a single blood test, as strenuous exercise increases the volume of plasma in the blood, diluting the levels of hemoglobin. This increase can sometimes incorrectly suggest there is a deficiency. This is called "sports anemia." It is not the same as iron-deficiency anemia—it is simply a consequence of endurance training. It does not need any treatment as it is generally found in people who are in the early stages of a training program.

OMEGA-3 FATTY ACIDS

Omega-3 fatty acids are important for normal blood vessel function, optimizing the delivery of oxygen to muscles, and improving aerobic capacity and endurance. They also help to speed up recovery and reduce inflammation and joint stiffness.

They form part of the structure of membranes of all cells, including red blood cells. A high intake of omega-3s will help make your red blood cells more flexible and allow them to move easily through blood capillaries and deliver oxygen efficiently to the muscles. Omega-3s are also necessary for proper brain function, hormone regulation, immune system function, and blood flow. They also help protect against heart disease and stroke, and may also help improve brain function, prevent Alzheimer's disease, treat depression, and help improve the behavior of children with dyslexia, dyspraxia, and ADHD. There are three main types of omega-3 fatty acids:

1   **EICOSAPENTAENOIC ACID (EPA)**—found in oily fish
2   **DOCOSAHEXAENOIC ACID (DHA**)—found in oily fish
3   **ALPHA-LINOLENIC ACID (ALA)**—found in plant foods, such as walnuts, rapeseed oil, pumpkin seeds, and flaxseed oil

FIVE TO FOCUS ON

1   NUTS, especially WALNUTS
2   RAPESEED OIL
3   SEEDS, especially PUMPKIN, FLAX, and CHIA SEEDS
4   FLAXSEED OIL
5   DARK GREEN LEAFY VEGETABLES

In the body ALA is converted to EPA and DHA, the two kinds of omega-3 fatty acids that can be more readily harnessed and used by the body. However, this process isn't very efficient—the body can only convert around 5–10 percent of the ALA you eat into EPA and 2-5 percent into DHA. So, unless you include plenty of ALA-rich foods in your diet, it's easy for vegetarians to fall short on EPA and DHA. Indeed, studies have shown that vegetarians have lower levels of DHA and EPA in their blood than non-vegetarians (Welch et al., 2010). The table on page 37 gives the omega-3 fatty acid content of various vegetarian foods.

Above: *Warm lentil salad with baby spinach and walnuts, page 93*
Left: *Super oat bars, page 175*

But, as well as ensuring you eat enough ALA, you also need to make sure you don't eat too many omega-6s (linoleic acid or LA), since a high intake of omega-6s interferes with the conversion process of ALA to EPA and DHA. Omega-6s are found in vegetable oils, such as sunflower, safflower, corn, and soy oil and most vegetable oil blends (typically labeled "vegetable oils"). Both omega-6s and omega-3s compete for the same conversion enzymes so eating too many omega-6s means the enzymes are not able to convert ALA into EPA and DHA. This can result in an imbalance of prostaglandins. These are hormone-like chemicals responsible for controlling blood clotting, inflammation, and the immune system. Over time, a high ratio of omega-6s to omega-3s may increase inflammation in the body, which is thought to be an underlying factor in chronic diseases such as cardiovascular disease, rheumatoid arthritis, and cancer. You should aim to achieve an LA to ALA ratio of around 4:1 or slightly lower. Minimize your use of oils high in omega-6s (i.e. corn, soy, safflower, sunflower, and most vegetable oil blends). Instead use low-omega-6 oils (i.e. olive and rapeseed oil), which do not disrupt the formation of EPA and DHA.

Walnut burgers, page 130

HOW MUCH DO YOU NEED?

There is no official recommended intake for omega-3s, but the Vegetarian Society recommends an ALA intake of 1.5 percent of energy, or roughly 4 g a day. This amount accounts for the low conversion rate of ALA to EPA and DHA. You can get this from:

- 1½ tsp flaxseed oil
- 2½ tbsp flaxseeds
- 1¼ tbsp chia seeds
- 3 tbsp rapeseed oil
- 1 handful (1.4 oz) walnuts

SHOULD VEGETARIAN ATHLETES TAKE SUPPLEMENTS?

It's a good idea to take vegetarian omega-3 supplements if you don't get food sources of omega-3s regularly. Opt for supplements made from algae oil—these are better options than those made from flaxseed oil as they contain high levels of both the omega-3 fatty acids DHA and EPA instead of ALA.

The high concentration of omega-3s found in oily fish is due to the algae they consume, which produces the oils.

HOW MUCH OMEGA-3?

FOOD	AMOUNT OF ALA
1 tablespoon flaxseed oil	7.2 g
1 tablespoon chia seeds	3.0 g
1 small handful (1 oz) walnuts	2.5 g
1 tablespoon hemp oil	2.1 g
1 small handful (1 oz) pumpkin seeds	2.1 g
1 tablespoon flaxseeds (ground)	1.6 g
1 tablespoon rapeseed oil	1.3 g
1 tablespoon soy oil	0.8 g
Tofu	0.6 g
1 capsule vegetarian omega-3 supplement (flaxseed oil)	0.6 g
2 capsules vegetarian omega-3 supplement (algal oil)	0.3 g*
2 omega-3 eggs**	0.3 g
3 tbsp (3.5 oz) broccoli	0.2 g
3 tbsp (3.5 oz) spinach	0.2 g
3 tbsp (3.5 oz) kale	0.2 g

*DHA and EPA, which is more potent than ALA
** Omega-3 eggs are from hens fed an omega-3-enriched diet

VITAMIN B$_{12}$

Vitamin B$_{12}$ is needed for making red blood cells and for the proper functioning of the nervous system. It also acts with folic acid and vitamin B$_6$ to control homocysteine levels. High levels of homocysteine are associated with an increased risk of heart disease. Consuming too little can result in fatigue, depression, and anemia (abnormal red blood cell development and shortness of breath) and nerve damage.

It is made in nature by micro-organisms so the only sources of vitamin B$_{12}$ are of animal origin (meat, dairy, and eggs). Vegetarians can get their daily quota from eggs and dairy products, but vegans will have to rely on B$_{12}$-fortified foods: non-dairy milks (e.g. soy, almond, and coconut milk), yeast extract or flakes, soy yogurt and cheese, soy burgers, and breakfast cereals, or take a supplement that provides B$_{12}$. Not all non-dairy milks are fortified with B$_{12}$ so check the ingredients listed on the label. Fermented foods such as tempeh and miso, shiitake mushrooms, seaweed, and algae contain chemically similar substances, but these do not have the same actions as B$_{12}$ in the body.

FIVE TO FOCUS ON

1   DAIRY PRODUCTS—milk, yogurt, and cheese
2   EGGS
3   FORTIFIED NON-DAIRY MILK
4   FORTIFIED YEAST EXTRACT (e.g. Marmite)
5   FORTIFIED BREAKFAST CEREALS

HOW MUCH DO YOU NEED?

Adults need 1.5 micrograms (mcg) of B_{12} daily. You can get this amount from:

- ¾ cup milk
- 1 large egg
- 18 oz yogurt
- 2 cups non-dairy milk
- 2½ portions (0.35 oz) fortified yeast extract (e.g. Marmite)
- 2 bowls (2.5 oz) fortified bran flakes

SHOULD VEGETARIAN ATHLETES TAKE SUPPLEMENTS?

If you eat dairy products and eggs, there's no need to take supplements. For vegans, the Vegetarian Society and Vegan Society recommend a multi-vitamin and mineral supplement that provides 10 mcg of B_{12}. Although this is considerably more than the official recommended intake, only a small percentage is absorbed—10 mcg in supplement form is equivalent to about 1 mcg from food.

HOW MUCH VITAMIN B_{12}?

FOOD	AMOUNT OF VITAMIN B_{12}
1 cup (7 oz) semi-skimmed milk	1.9 mcg
1 egg	1.4 mcg
1 pot (4.5 oz) plain low-fat yogurt	0.4 mcg
1 slice (1 oz) Cheddar cheese	0.6 mcg
1 cup (7 oz) fortified almond milk	0.8 mcg
1 cup (7 oz) fortified soy milk	0.8 mcg
1 cup (7 oz) fortified coconut milk	0.8 mcg
1 pot (4.5 oz) fortified soy yogurt	0.5 mcg
1 serving (0.15 oz) yeast extract (e.g. Marmite)	0.6 mcg
1 small bowl (1 oz) fortified bran flakes	0.6 mcg
1 small serving (1 oz) Ready Brek	0.6 mcg
1 soy burger (2.5 oz)	0.8 mcg

CALCIUM

Calcium is needed for strong, healthy bones and teeth. It also helps with blood clotting and nerve and muscle function. Low intakes over time may result in weak bones and increase your risk of stress fractures and brittle bones (osteoporosis). Obtaining sufficient amounts of calcium can be more difficult if you don't consume milk or dairy foods, as these foods are rich in calcium. Also, it is in a form that is particularly well absorbed by the body compared with plant foods. Indeed, surveys show that vegans consume less calcium than people who include dairy products.

Vegan sources include fortified non-dairy milk (e.g. soy, almond, and coconut), tofu, almonds, dried figs, dark green vegetables, beans, lentils, chia seeds, and sesame seeds. Broccoli, kale, Tuscan kale, bok choy, and watercress are good options for vegans, as they provide not only good levels of calcium but also vitamin K, potassium, and magnesium, which contribute to bone health.

FIVE TO FOCUS ON

1 DAIRY PRODUCTS—milk, yogurt, and cheese
2 TOFU
3 FORTIFIED NON-DAIRY MILK
4 FIGS
5 RED KIDNEY BEANS

HOW MUCH DO YOU NEED?

The recommended intake for adults is 700 mg daily, which you can get from three servings of dairy products.

SHOULD VEGETARIAN ATHLETES TAKE SUPPLEMENTS?

Consider supplementing your diet with up to 800 mg a day if you don't eat many calcium-rich foods. Be warned: Taking more than the recommended daily dose of calcium on a regular basis could lead to heart problems and kidney stones, and interfere with the absorption of other minerals such as iron and magnesium.

HOW MUCH CALCIUM?

FOOD	AMOUNT OF CALCIUM
3.5 oz tofu	510 mg
1 cup (7 oz) semi-skimmed milk	240 mg
1 cup (7 oz) fortified soy or almond milk	240 mg
4 ready-to-eat dried figs (3.5 oz)	230 mg
1 pot (4.5 oz) low-fat plain yogurt	200 mg
1 slice (1 oz) Cheddar cheese	185 mg
4 heaped tbsp. (9 oz) cooked red kidney beans (75 g dry weight)	140 mg
3 tbsp (3.5 oz) kale	130 mg
4 tbsp (9 oz) cooked chickpeas	86 mg
1 small handful (1 oz) almonds	60 mg
2-3 florets (2.8 oz) broccoli	56 mg
3 tbsp (3.5 oz) bok choy	54 mg

VITAMIN D

For many years the main benefit of vitamin D was thought to be that it helped us absorb calcium from our food and keep our bones strong and healthy. However, we now know that vitamin D has many other roles in the body, including:

- Muscle function
- Supporting the health of the immune system, brain, and nervous system
- Regulating insulin levels
- Supporting lung function and cardiovascular health
- Influence the expression of genes involved in cancer development

Receptors for vitamin D have been found in almost all tissues in the body. This means that it acts within these cells, affecting a large number of body systems. It is also needed for optimal performance and immune function. Low levels may reduce muscle function and strength, and may also increase the risk of injury and illness. Low levels have been associated with reduced performance while high levels may enhance performance. According to one study, as many as 62 percent of UK athletes have insufficient or deficient levels of serum vitamin D, defined as less than 50 ng/ml (Close et al., 2013).

It is also thought that vitamin D may protect against several chronic diseases, including heart disease, dementia, bowel cancer, and type 2 diabetes, although the exact connection isn't yet clear.

Around 90 percent of our vitamin D comes from exposure to ultraviolet B (UVB) radiation. Blood levels typically fall during winter months, as the sunlight doesn't have enough UVB radiation. From April to September in the northern hemisphere, you should be able to get all the vitamin D you need from 15 minutes of sun exposure a day on your face and arms.

There are relatively few vegetarian food sources of this vitamin. These include egg yolks, sun-exposed mushrooms, and fortified foods such as margarine, non-dairy milks, and breakfast cereals. Much like our skin, mushrooms have the capacity to produce vitamin D when exposed to ultraviolet light, even after they've been picked. You can do this at home: just place mushrooms on a plate or tray and leave them in a sunny spot for about half an hour. You'll greatly increase the vitamin D content.

HOW MUCH DO YOU NEED?

The National Institutes of Health recommend 15 micrograms (mcg) or 600 IU (international units) daily.

SHOULD VEGETARIAN ATHLETES TAKE SUPPLEMENTS?

Supplements may be a good idea during the winter months when vitamin D levels tend to be low. The National Institutes of Health and Clinical Excellence (NICE) advises taking 10 mcg (400 IU) vitamin D a day for the under 5s, people over 65, and those who have low or no exposure to the sun.

HOW MUCH VITAMIN D?

FOOD	AMOUNT OF VITAMIN D
2 eggs	3.2 mcg
1 cup (7 oz) soy or other non-dairy milk (fortified)	1.5 mcg
1 small bowl (1 oz) bran flakes (fortified)	1.3 mcg
1 small bowl (1 oz) Ready Brek (fortified)	1.3 mcg
1 pot (4.5 oz) soy yogurt (fortified)	0.9 mcg
1 portion (½ oz) olive oil, sunflower or soy spread (fortified)	0.8 mcg
1 slice (1 oz) cheese	0.1 mcg
1 portion (½ oz) butter	0.1 mcg

HOW TO MAXIMIZE PERFORMANCE WITHOUT MEAT

Following a healthy diet with adequate amounts of energy, carbohydrates, protein, vitamins, and minerals is critical for optimal performance. Now you know which nutrients and foods you need to focus on, the next step is planning your diet around your exercise schedule. What and how much you eat around training can make a big difference to difference to how you feel and also to your stamina, strength, and power. Choosing the wrong foods, eating too much or too little, or eating at the wrong time can affect your performance and leave you feeling hungry, uncomfortable, or unwell. Eating the right foods at the right time ensures that you will be able to perform at your best.

PRE-EXERCISE NUTRITION

The ideal time for a pre-exercise meal is 2 to 4 hours before your workout because it's early enough to digest the food, yet late enough that this energy won't be used up by the time you begin exercising. In a study at the University of North Carolina, athletes who ate 3 hours before a run were able to exercise longer than those who ate 6 hours beforehand (Maffucci & McMurray, 2000).

Eating a meal too close to training could make you feel uncomfortable, "heavy," and nauseous as the blood supply diverts from the stomach and digestive organs to the muscles to provide the necessary energy for muscular work. That's why stomach cramps and stomach aches are the most common complaints when trying to run on a full stomach. The body is not designed to digest a big meal and exercise at the same time!

On the other hand, leaving too long a gap means you may feel hungry and lightheaded during exercise and lacking energy. The closer your pre-workout meal is to your workout, the smaller it must be. If you have only a couple of hours before your workout, then eat a small meal of 300 to 400 calories. No time for a meal? Then have a small snack (e.g. bananas, plain yogurt, or porridge) or a smoothie 30 to 60 minutes beforehand. It's a myth that eating during the hour before exercise results in low blood sugar levels or hypoglycemia (Jeukendrup & Killer, 2010). If you are able to eat 4 hours before your workout then you can probably eat a larger meal of 600 to 800 calories, or approximately 10 calories/kg body weight. You should feel comfortable at the start of your workout, neither hungry nor full.

In practice, the exact timing of your pre-exercise meal will probably depend on constraints such as work hours, travel, and session times. Try to plan meals as best you can around these commitments. For example, if you work out at 7 o'clock, plan to eat a substantial lunch followed by a small (300–400 calories) pre-exercise meal at 5 o'clock. If you prefer training at 5 o'clock, then eat your pre-exercise meal (lunch) at 1 o'clock followed by a snack of 100 to 300 calories, 30 to 60 minutes before your workout if you're feeling hungry.

If you train first thing in the morning, having a carbohydrate-based meal or snack an hour before you head off will increase your endurance and performance. Try porridge, toast, wholegrain cereal, or a banana. Always have a drink—water is the best choice. You will have lost a lot of fluid in the night and need to rehydrate before training. If you cannot face solid food first thing, a smoothie or fruit juice (diluted by half with water) will provide energy to fuel your muscles during training. Persevere—you will soon get used to the feeling of food and drink in your stomach early in the morning and find that you'll be able to train harder and longer. Another option is to have a larger supper the night before and then a drink prior to your early morning session.

Around 60 to 80 percent of the calories in your pre-exercise meal or snack should come from carbohydrates. The carbohydrates in this meal will help maintain blood sugar levels during your workout and aid performance. Indeed, many studies have shown eating a carbohydrate-rich diet before exercise increases endurance and performance. Conversely, an inadequate carbohydrate intake results in low muscle stores and reduced endurance.

You should also include some protein (such as cheese, egg, milk, yogurt, beans, lentils, or nuts) in your pre-workout meal. This will produce a more gradual and sustained rise in blood sugar as well as help reduce muscle breakdown during exercise, and improve performance. Avoid fried food or fat-heavy meals as fat delays digestion and may make you feel uncomfortable during training.

Above: *Chickpea and vegetable tagine, page 114*
Opposite: *Fruit and nut bars, page 176*

PRE-TRAINING MEALS

- Baked potato with cheese or baked beans plus salad
- Pasta with tomato and vegetable sauce, cheese; plus vegetables
- Porridge with bananas and raisins
- Lentil, quinoa, and bean bake (page 116)
- Chickpea and vegetable tagine with couscous (page 114)
- Lentil and rice pilaf (page 104)
- Tofu noodles (page 141)
- Butter beans with butternut squash and spinach (page 100)

PRE-TRAINING SNACKS

If you don't have time for a meal, have a snack 30 minutes before training with a drink of water.

- Bananas
- A handful of dried fruit and nuts
- A smoothie
- Avocado toast (page 194)
- Fruit and nut bars (page 176)
- Raw energy bars (page 170)
- Super oat bars (page 175)
- Date and cashew bars (page 171)

The theory behind this is that by not eating before a workout—and exercising with lower blood glucose levels—it forces the muscles to burn proportionally more calories from fat and less from carbohydrate. While this is true up to a point, it doesn't mean you'll shed weight faster. Exercising with low blood glucose levels can induce early fatigue, which results in an overall lower calorie burn. Also, skipping a pre-workout meal or snack may leave you so hungry that you overeat after the session. What matters is your daily energy balance: consuming fewer calories than you burn throughout the day.

HYDRATION

It's crucial that you are fully hydrated before you begin training, otherwise you risk dehydration early in the session. This can affect your stamina, speed, and performance, and cause early fatigue, headache, nausea, and dizziness.

Prevention is better than cure. If you train in the evening, ensure you drink plenty of water during the day. If you train early in the morning, have a drink upon rising. You will know if you are properly hydrated from the color of your urine. It should be pale straw-colored, not deep yellow, and should not have a strong odor. You can make up for any previously incurred fluid deficits by consuming 12 to 17 oz about four hours before training, and continuing to drink little and often.

For workouts lasting less than an hour, water is the best choice. It is absorbed rapidly and hydrates the body. For longer sessions, consuming extra carbohydrate in the form of a drink (e.g. juice or a sports drink) will also help maintain blood glucose levels and fuel the muscles. Alternatively, you may prefer consuming water plus food (e.g. bananas, raisins, or energy gels).

Current advice is to drink when you are thirsty and listen to your body. For most workouts and climates, 13.5–27 oz per hour will prevent dehydration as well as over-hydration. Aim to consume fluids at a rate that keeps pace with your sweat rate. You'll sweat more in hot and humid conditions and when working out harder.

NUTRITION DURING EXERCISE

For endurance workouts lasting longer than one hour, consuming extra carbohydrates can help you maintain your pace and keep going longer. Aim to consume between 30 and 60 g per hour in the form of a drink or as solid food. The following supply 30 g carbohydrates:

- 1 cup fruit juice
- 2 cups isotonic sports drink
- 1½ bananas
- 2 x 1 oz energy gels
- ¼ cup raisins
- ¼ cup soft (ready-to-eat) dried apricots
- 2 date and cashew bars (page 171)
- 6 gummy bears
- 4 energy chews

If you're exercising longer than 2½ hours (e.g. ultra-distance running, triathlon, cycling, or marathon), then consuming up to 90 g carbohydrate per hour will help sustain your performance and delay fatigue. Ideally this should be a mixture of 2 parts glucose to 1 part fructose, which you can get from dual-energy source sports drinks or gels. Dual-energy means it contains two types of carbohydrates, usually a mixture of glucose (or maltodextrin) and fructose. Maltodextrin is a type of carbohydrate (comprising short chains of glucose molecules) made from corn starch.

RECOVERY NUTRITION

What you eat and drink after a workout is critical when it comes to speeding muscle recovery and improving your fitness. For speediest recovery, focus on these three key stages.

REHYDRATION

Replacing lost fluids is the priority as your muscles cannot fully recover until your cells are properly hydrated. The exact amount you need to drink depends on how dehydrated you are after your workout. The "pee test" will give you an idea how dehydrated you are; otherwise weigh yourself before and after training. For each 2.2 lb of body weight lost, drink 50 oz of fluid (e.g. water, diluted juice, or milk). Replacing lost fluid takes time and is best achieved by drinking little and often. Drinking a large volume in one go stimulates urine formation, so much of the fluid is lost rather than retained.

REFUEL AND REBUILD

You need to replace the fuel (glycogen) that you've used before your next session by consuming carbohydrates and also rebuild damaged muscle by consuming protein. If you have less than 24 hours before your next workout (i.e. you train twice a day), then you need to take advantage of the 2-hour recovery window— this is when your muscles restock glycogen and rebuild proteins faster than normal. However, if you have 24 hours or longer between workouts, then the timing of your post-workout meal is less critical. There's no particular advantage in eating immediately after exercise. Just eat your post-workout meal when you feel hungry for it. Provided you consume sufficient calories, carbohydrates, and protein over a 24-hour period, your muscles will recover before your next workout.

Include the right balance of carbohydrates and protein in your post-workout snack or meal. The combination of these two nutrients promotes faster muscle repair and greater muscle growth, and reduces post-exercise muscle soreness. Your post-workout meal or snack should, ideally, comprise about 20 g protein or about 0.25 g per kilogram of body weight (Moore et al., 2009). As muscle recovery continues for several hours, include about 20 g protein in each meal (Moore et al., 2012). Eating more than this will not increase muscle growth or speed recovery. The breakfast main meal recipes in Part 2 all provide approximately 20 g per serving.

Opt for "real" food rather than commercial recovery drinks— these lack fiber, phytochemicals, and other health-protective nutrients of real foods. Also, foods such as milk, yogurt, fresh and dried fruit, nuts, and wholegrain toast offer considerable money savings compared with recovery products foods.

Here are seven of the best foods for muscle recovery that provide nutrients in amounts that optimize muscle recovery after a hard session:

1   3 TABLESPOONS OF ALMONDS OR CASHEWS PLUS ⅔ CUP STRAINED GREEK YOGURT—Nuts not only supply protein but also vitamin E, iron, and fiber. Strained Greek yogurt is more concentrated so contains about twice the protein of ordinary yogurt.

2   2 CUPS MILK WITH A BANANA—Any type of milk will provide the protein needed to maximize muscle adaptation after exercise. It also contains the optimal amount of the amino acid leucine to promote muscle building after exercise.

3   1 OUNCE OF TART CHERRY JUICE CONCENTRATE—Studies show that muscle recovery is significantly faster compared to a placebo, thanks to its high levels of antioxidant flavonoid compounds.

4   A BOWL OF PORRIDGE WITH NUTS AND FRUIT—Made with 1 ¾ cups milk and ½ cup oats, porridge is an ideal muscle recovery food after early morning training, as it provides the perfect ratio of carbohydrates and protein, along with B-vitamins, iron, and fiber.

5   ALMOND AND PUMPKIN SEED OAT BARS (page 181)—An ideal alternative to shop-bought oat bars, these provide more protein, omega-3 fats, and iron.

6   STRAWBERRY RECOVERY SHAKE (page 196) or banana and peanut butter shake (page 199)—An excellent mixture of protein, carbohydrates, and those all-important phytochemicals.

7   DATE AND CASHEW BARS (page 171)—Packed with protein, essential fats, vitamins, and minerals to repair and rebuild muscle.

Recovery continues well past the immediate post-exercise period, so you need to continue paying attention to your diet and fluid intake. Protein manufacture increases over the following 24 to 48 hours, generally peaking after about 24 hours. If you don't supply your body with adequate nutrients, you risk incomplete recovery and sub-par adaptation to training. Eat regularly spaced nutritious meals that deliver protein and carbohydrate along with fiber, vitamins, minerals, and healthy fats. Try Dhal with butternut squash and spinach (page 108), Potato, spinach and goat cheese frittata (page 138), Spiced quinoa and tofu pilaf (page 145), or Red lentil shepherd's pie (page 128).

Left: *Banana and cinnamon porridge*
Right: *Chocolate and peanut butter porridge*
pages 52 and 53

NOTES

■ All the recipes are vegetarian, but always check all ingredients (e.g. cheese and condiments) are suitable for vegetarians.
■ **VG** This indicates the recipe is vegan.
■ Many recipes can be adapted to make them vegan by substituting non-dairy milk (e.g. soy, coconut, almond, rice, or oat milk) or yogurt.

PART 2

The recipes

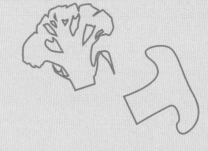

My aim in this section is to help you put vegetarian nutrition into practice and show you that vegetarian cooking can be easy, tasty, and exciting. Gone are the days when vegetarian cooking meant boring omelettes, salads, or a bowl of lentils. With so many ingredients available nowadays, there are limitless possibilities of color and flavor combinations. Vegetarian cooking need never be dull! These recipes show how to combine fantastic, fresh ingredients to make amazing breakfasts, main meals, soups, salads, desserts, snacks, and smoothies all bursting with delicious flavor. And they're all fast food—most can be prepared in less than 30 minutes.

The key to a healthy vegetarian diet is substituting a variety of alternative protein sources, such as beans, lentils, tofu, and nuts in place of meat and fish. The next priority is to include plant sources of iron and omega-3 fats, two nutrients that vegetarians sometimes fall down on (for more on this, see pages 31–37). This can be easily achieved by making beans, lentils, nuts, and seeds the focus of your main meals. After that, add plenty of vegetables—at least two types per meal—and eat a rainbow of colors to get a wide range of nutrients.

You'll see that the recipes in this section are all simple and quick to make, requiring no complicated cooking skills or techniques. The recipes are all designed with the specific nutritional needs of athletes in mind. So, they combine nutritious ingredients that provide the ideal balance of protein, carbohydrates, and essential fats for performance and recovery. The inclusion of plenty of fresh and colorful produce means that each recipe is also packed with nutrients that assist with energy production, muscle building, and healthy immune function.

I'm mindful that calorie needs of athletes vary considerably (depending on your sport and training program) so you may need anything from 2,000 calories a day to more than 4,000 calories a day. Most of the main meal recipes serve two, but use the quantities simply as a guide. You can adjust the quantities if you want bigger or smaller portions, or if you are cooking for a different number of people. Each recipe provides a nutritional breakdown so you can see how it contributes to your daily calorie and nutritional intake.

In the following pages you'll find more than 100 recipes suitable for everyday meals and snacks that have all been tried and tested by family members and close friends. These recipes have fueled my own sporting success as a national bodybuilding champion, as well as that of my husband (a competitive masters runner) and two daughters (both national swimmers). I hope that you will enjoy these recipes as much I do, and discover that vegetarian meals can be both healthy and delicious. And you'll see that you really can build muscle without meat!

CHAPTER 3

BREKFASTS

BREAKFASTS

Clockwise from top right: *Blueberry porridge, Egg and avocado toast, Fruit and nut muesli, Blueberry oat pancakes*

BANANA AND CINNAMON PORRIDGE

Full of slow-release carbs, porridge is the perfect way to start the day. Add some cinnamon
and throw in a banana and some nuts and make it much tastier (and healthier).
Ring the changes with a handful of raisins, a few chopped dates or dried apricots,
a spoonful of shredded, unsweetened coconut or apple purée—whatever takes your fancy!

½ cup (2 oz) rolled oats

1¼ cups (10 fl oz) any milk of your choice

A pinch of cinnamon

1 banana, sliced

1 tbsp chopped nuts (e.g. almonds,
walnuts, or pecans)

Serves 1

Mix the oats, milk, and half the sliced banana in a saucepan.
Bring to a boil, turn down the heat to a simmer, and cook for
4–5 minutes, stirring frequently. Stir in the cinnamon.

Serve topped with the nuts and remaining banana.

NUTRITION per serving:
- 501 cals • 22 g protein • 14 g fat (2 g saturates)
- 69 g carbs (39 g total sugars) • 6 g fiber

CHOCOLATE AND PEANUT BUTTER PORRIDGE (VG)

If you're a peanut butter fan like me, then you'll love this yummy twist on basic porridge. A spoonful of cocoa and peanut butter (or even almond butter) transforms it into a chocolatey bowl of deliciousness. And it's also a brilliant way of boosting your protein, iron, B vitamins, and fiber intake.

1/2 cup (2 oz) rolled oats
1 1/4 cups (10 fl oz) any milk of your choice
1 tsp cocoa powder (or more if you like)
1 tbsp peanut butter (I use crunchy)
A pinch of cinnamon
1 banana, sliced

Optional:
Drizzle of honey or maple syrup
Plain yogurt

Serves 1

Put the oats, milk, and cocoa powder in a pan over medium heat. When it starts to bubble, turn down the heat. Enjoy the gorgeous chocolate aroma! Stir until the porridge thickens and the oats are cooked, about 4–5 minutes.

Stir in the peanut butter and cinnamon, spoon into bowls, top with banana slices, and, if you like, a drizzle of honey or maple syrup and a dollop of yogurt.

> **NUTRITION per serving:**
> • 520 cals • 23 g protein • 15 g fat (3 g saturates)
> • 70 g carbs (39 g total sugars) • 8 g fiber

Blueberry porridge

BLUEBERRY PORRIDGE

We call this "purple porridge" in our house! It's not only a beautiful color but is also full of purpley goodness! Blueberries are real powerhouses of nutrients—rich in polyphenols and vitamin C, both of which help increase exercise performance and promote speedy recovery. Adding them to porridge is a surefire way to boost your next workout.

¹/₂ cup (2 oz) rolled oats

1 ¹/₄ cups (10 fl oz) any milk of your choice

A handful of fresh or frozen blueberries (defrosted)

A pinch of cinnamon

Half a banana, sliced

Drizzle of honey or maple syrup, to taste

Optional: A few drops of vanilla extract

Serves 1

Put the oats and milk into a large pan and bring to a boil. Turn down the heat, add the blueberries, and cook over a medium heat, stirring occasionally until the porridge thickens and the oats are cooked, about 4-5 minutes. The porridge will turn a dark shade of purple! Stir in the cinnamon and vanilla.

Once you have the consistency you want (I prefer my porridge really thick!), pour the porridge into a bowl. It thickens more the longer it cooks, so for a thinner consistency cook for a shorter time. Top with a few extra blueberries, the banana slices, and a drizzle of honey or maple syrup.

NUTRITION per serving:
- 415 cals • 18 g protein • 6 g fat (1 g saturates)
- 70 g carbs (36 g total sugars) • 8 g fiber

MICROWAVE PORRIDGE

If you don't always have time to make proper porridge on the stove, here is a shortcut when you only have 3 minutes. It tastes almost as good and is just as healthy.

¹/₂ cup (2 oz) rolled oats

¹/₂ tsp cinnamon or vanilla extract

1 ¹/₄ cups any milk of your choice

Optional ingredients: Banana slices, honey or maple syrup, raisins, chopped dates or nuts

Serves 1

Mix the oats, cinnamon or vanilla, and milk in bowl (use a large bowl to prevent spilling over when cooking). Cook in the microwave on full power for 1½ minutes, stir, then microwave for another 1½ minutes. Stir again.

Top with any extra ingredients (see left).

NUTRITION per serving:
- 288 cals • 16 g protein • 5 g fat (1 g saturates)
- 42 g carbs (14 g total sugars) • 5 g fiber

FRUIT AND NUT MUESLI

I'm fussy when it comes to muesli and dislike it served straight from the packet with milk.
It may be very healthy but most varieties taste like cardboard and require so much chewing.
So here's a delicious and even healthier alternative that's soaked in yogurt overnight in the fridge.
The muesli absorbs the liquid, giving a softer and altogether more pleasant texture!

1/3 cup (1 1/2 oz) basic muesli
1 cup low-fat plain Greek yogurt
1 tbsp dried fruit e.g. raisins, golden raisins, apricots, or dates
1 tbsp sliced almonds (or any other variety of nuts or seeds)
A generous handful of berries, e.g. strawberries, raspberries, or blueberries
Optional: A little honey
Serves 1

In a bowl, mix together the muesli, yogurt, dried fruit, and nuts. Cover and leave for at least 30 minutes or overnight (up to 3 days) in the fridge.

Stir in the berries and serve with a drizzle of honey, if you like.

NUTRITION per serving:
• 467 cals, 36 g protein • 12 g fat (1 g saturates)
• 51 g carbs (31 g total sugars) • 8 g fiber

BIRCHER MUESLI WITH RASPBERRIES

This easy-to-make recipe makes the perfect post-workout breakfast as it contains the ideal 3:1 ratio of carbohydrates to protein to refuel depleted muscles. The high polyphenol and vitamin C content of the raspberries helps reduce muscle damage and inflammation and promotes recovery; while the walnuts supply valuable omega-3s.

3/4 cup low-fat plain Greek yogurt
1/4 cup oats
1 tbsp golden raisins
1 small apple, grated
1/3 cup raspberries
1/2 small banana, sliced
A drizzle of honey
A few chopped walnuts
Serves 1

In a small bowl, mix together the yogurt, oats, and golden raisins. Cover and leave overnight in the fridge.

To serve, stir in the grated apple, raspberries, and banana slices; drizzle with the honey and scatter the chopped walnuts.

NUTRITION per serving:
• 468 cals • 23 g protein • 13 g fat (2 g saturates)
• 61 g carbs (46 g total sugars) • 8 g fiber

Fruit and nut muesli

Overnight oats with blueberries

OVERNIGHT OATS WITH BLUEBERRIES

Overnight oats are essentially oats soaked overnight in yogurt or milk. The idea is that the oats absorb the liquid and soften, creating an instant breakfast (rather like cold porridge) that can be eaten straight from the fridge in the morning. You can make it in a bowl or in a wide-neck jar (or other food container) that you can pop in your kit bag or handbag and take with you to the gym or work in the morning. Make a batch—the mixture will keep in the fridge for up to two days and it makes a great pre- or post-workout snack.

1/2 cup rolled oats

A pinch of cinnamon

1/3 cup low-fat plain Greek yogurt

1/2 cup any milk of your choice

1–2 tsp maple syrup or honey, to taste

A handful of blueberries

A few walnuts

Optional mix-in ingredients: Peanut butter, protein powder, chopped apple, cinnamon or vanilla extract

Serves 1

Mix together the oats, cinnamon, yogurt, milk, maple syrup or honey, and blueberries in a bowl or a glass jar. Cover and put in the fridge overnight so the oats absorb all the liquid.

In the morning, remove from the fridge, top with the walnuts, and enjoy!

NUTRITION per serving:
• 420 cals • 20 g protein • 14 g fat (2 g saturates)
• 49 g carbs (22 g total sugars) • 7 g fiber

OVERNIGHT OATS WITH BANANA

This variation of overnight oats includes banana, which provides natural sweetness, and chia seeds, which help thicken the mixture. The seeds are rich in omega-3 fats, fiber, and protein, and, unlike flax seeds, don't have to be ground to be absorbed by the body. And the toppings are endless!

1/2 cup rolled oats

1/3 cup low-fat plain Greek yogurt

1/2 cup any milk of your choice

1 tbsp chia seeds

A pinch of cinnamon

1 banana, sliced

Optional toppings: Toasted sliced almonds, fresh blackberries, raspberries, or strawberries

Serves 1

Mix together the oats, yogurt, milk, chia seeds, cinnamon, and sliced banana in a bowl. Cover and put in the fridge overnight so the oats absorb all the yogurt.

In the morning, remove from the fridge. Scatter sliced almonds and top with fresh fruit (optional). You can also add extra milk or yogurt if you like.

NUTRITION per serving:
• 418 cals • 21 g protein • 9 g fat (1 g saturates)
• 58 g carbs (33 g total sugars) • 10 g fiber

BLUEBERRY OAT PANCAKES

These pancakes are far healthier than ordinary pancakes as they are made with oats and bananas instead of flour so contain more protein and fiber. They're packed with yummy blueberries so they're bursting with polyphenols and vitamin C. Make a batch, freeze, and thaw in a microwave for a quick breakfast when you're pressed for time.

1 cup rolled oats

1 tsp baking powder

1 banana, mashed

2 eggs

$^2/_3$ cup any milk of your choice

A little light olive oil, rapeseed oil, or butter

2 cups blueberries

Optional toppings: A few crushed pecans, a little honey or maple syrup, extra blueberries, banana slices

Makes 8 (approx.)

In a bowl, mix together the oats and baking powder. Mix the mashed banana with the eggs and milk (you can do this with a hand blender if you prefer). Mix the banana mixture into the flour.

Heat a nonstick pan on medium heat, add a little oil or butter. Drop large spoonfuls of batter onto the pan and cook until bubbles form and the edges are cooked. Scatter a handful of blueberries and flip the pancake over. Cook for another couple of minutes on the other side. Repeat with the remaining batter.

Serve the pancakes topped with crushed pecans, a little honey or maple syrup, or some extra blueberries and banana slices.

NUTRITION per pancake:
- 113 cals • 4 g protein • 4 g fat (1 g saturates)
- 15 g carbs (6 g total sugars) • 2 g fiber

HOW TO TOAST NUTS

Nuts on their own are delicious and healthy. But toasting the nuts really brings out their "nutty" flavor. To toast nuts in the oven, spread them in an even layer on a baking sheet and place in the oven at 350 °F for 10 to 15 minutes. Check them often and stir halfway through the cooking time to make sure all the nuts are toasting evenly. Alternatively, toast in a dry frying pan over a medium-high heat, stirring frequently until they are golden brown and smell amazing.

APPLE CINNAMON OAT PANCAKES

These scrumptious pancakes provide a near-perfect combination of protein (egg and milk) and slow-release carbohydrates (oats and apple) to sustain you throughout the morning. They are amazingly fluffy and light, and super-easy to make.

1 cup rolled oats

1 tsp baking powder

½–1 tsp cinnamon

2 eggs

⅔ cup any milk of your choice

1 apple, grated

A little light olive oil, rapeseed oil, or butter

To serve: Drizzle of honey or maple syrup

Makes 8 (approx.)

Place all the ingredients except the oil/butter in a blender and process until well combined. Alternatively, mix together the dry ingredients in a bowl, then add the eggs, milk, and grated apple.

Heat a large nonstick pan on medium heat, add a little oil or butter. Drop large spoonfuls of batter onto the pan and cook for about 1 to 1½ minutes until bubbles form and the edges are cooked. Flip the pancake over with a thin spatula and cook for another 1 to 1½ minutes on the other side. Repeat with the remaining batter.

NUTRITION per pancake:
• 87 cals • 4 g protein • 4 g fat (1 g saturates)
• 10 g carbs (2 g total sugars) • 1 g fiber

QUICK BANANA PANCAKES

These are a firm favorite in my house. When you mix bananas and eggs together they magically turn into amazing pancakes—exactly like ordinary pancakes but with a softer texture. Add a handful of colorful berries and a dollop of Greek yogurt and you've got pretty much the perfect pre- or post-workout combo.

2 bananas

3 eggs

A little light olive oil, rapeseed oil, or butter

To serve: A handful of blackberries, strawberries, or raspberries or low-fat plain Greek yogurt

Optional batter ingredients: ¼ tsp baking powder (to make fluffier pancakes), 1 tsp cinnamon or vanilla extract, 1 tbsp raisins, a few chopped walnuts, 1 tbsp peanut butter

Makes 8

Mash the bananas in a bowl. Aim for a fairly smooth texture for a more authentic-looking pancake. Add the eggs and mix together until well combined. Alternatively, mix in a blender and process until fairly smooth.

Heat a large nonstick pan on medium heat, add a little oil or butter. Drop spoonfuls of batter onto the pan and cook for 30–45 seconds. Flip the pancake over with a thin spatula and cook for another 15–30 seconds on the other side. Repeat with the remaining batter.

NUTRITION per pancake:
• 66 cals • 3 g protein • 3 g fat (1 g saturates)
• 7 g carbs (6 total sugars) • 1 g fiber

PERFECT SCRAMBLED EGGS

Eggs are high in protein and contain all the amino acids needed for muscle growth and repair. They are also good sources of iron and vitamin B$_{12}$, two nutrients that can be in short supply in vegetarian diets. Here's my healthy take on the breakfast classic. I've replaced the butter and cream in the traditional version with yogurt, which dramatically lowers the saturated fat content of the dish but retains all the lovely creamy texture.

2 eggs

2 tsp low-fat plain Greek yogurt

A little salt and freshly ground black pepper

2 slices wholegrain or rye bread

Optional toppings: Halved cherry tomatoes, chopped spring onion, avocado slices, baby spinach

Serves 1

Crack the eggs into a bowl, add the yogurt and seasoning, and mix well.

Add the egg mixture to a hot, nonstick pan over medium heat and stir continuously with a wooden spoon until the eggs begin to set—this will take 2–3 minutes. Remove them from the heat when they are almost set, as they continue cooking for a short while.

While the eggs are cooking, toast the bread. Serve the scrambled eggs on top of the toast with extra black pepper.

NUTRITION per serving:
• 349 cals • 23 g protein • 3 g fat (3 g saturates)
• 33 g carbs (2 g total sugars) • 6 g fiber

EGG AND AVOCADO TOAST

Avocado toast or "avo toast" has become quite a "thing" in the fitness world. And by that I mean it's a good thing! It's literally smashed avocado on a slice of toast—quick, healthy, and delicious. Add a poached egg and you have a perfectly balanced breakfast that's rich in protein, monounsaturated fats, carbohydrates, and fiber. It's also a good way of getting your iron. Jazz it up with any of the suggested toppings.

2 eggs

2 slices wholegrain bread

½ avocado

Sea salt flakes and freshly ground pepper

Fresh or dried herbs (parsley, thyme or basil)

Optional toppings: A few halved cherry tomatoes, a pinch of red chili flakes, a little peanut butter underneath the avocado, or a few crushed pistachios or pine nuts

Serves 1

Bring a pan of water to boil (use enough water to cover the eggs). Crack an egg into a cup, then slip it into the water. Alternatively, crack the egg into a silicone egg poacher and place this in the boiling water. Turn down the heat and poach for about 4 minutes until the white is just set.

While the eggs are cooking, toast the bread and, using a fork, roughly smash the avocado on each piece of toast. When the eggs are cooked, use a slotted spoon to lift the eggs out of the water and place on top of the toast. Sprinkle with salt, freshly ground black pepper, and herbs.

NUTRITION per serving:
• 488 cals • 22 g protein • 28 g fat (6 g saturates)
• 33 g carbs (3 g total sugars) • 9 g fiber

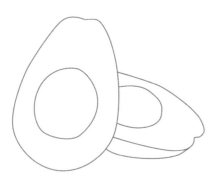

CHAPTER 4

SOUPS

· ·

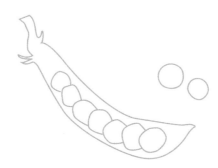

Clockwise from top right: *Butternut squash soup, Seriously green soup,
Red lentil vegetable soup and Ultimate vegetable soup*

ULTIMATE VEGETABLE SOUP

This vegetable soup is packed full of healthy vegetables and herbs. The beauty of the recipe is that you can substitute any other seasonal veg, such as butternut squash, red peppers, or leeks. Whatever you decide, it's a delicious way of getting your 5-a-day.

1 tbsp light olive or rapeseed oil

1 onion, finely sliced

1 carrot, sliced

1 small parsnip, diced

2 cups vegetable stock
(2 tsp vegetable bouillon)

1 bay leaf

³/₄ cup green beans,
trimmed and halved

2 cups green veg, e.g. kale,
cabbage, or spring greens

A small handful basil leaves, roughly torn

Salt and freshly ground black pepper

Serves 2

Heat the olive oil in a heavy-bottomed saucepan over moderate heat. Add the onion and cook gently for about 5 minutes until softened.

Add the carrots and parsnips to the pan and continue cooking over moderate heat for 5 minutes, stirring occasionally, until the vegetables soften a little.

Add the stock and bay leaf and bring to a boil. Simmer for 10 minutes, add the beans and greens, and cook for a further 5 minutes.

Remove and discard the bay leaf. Liquidize the soup using a blender. Stir in the basil and season with salt and freshly ground pepper.

NUTRITION per serving:
- 176 cals • 5 g protein • 8 g fat (1 g saturates)
- 16 g carbs (10 g total sugars) • 10 g fiber

MOROCCAN-STYLE LENTIL SOUP

This is a brilliant soup for when the weather gets a bit nippy. It's a decent source of protein and fiber, as well as B vitamins and potassium. You can use any lentils for this but traditionally brown ones are used.

1 tbsp light olive or rapeseed oil
1 small onion, sliced
1 leek, sliced
1 carrot, sliced
1 celery stalk, thinly sliced
1 potato, diced
2 cups vegetable stock
¼ cup brown or Puy lentils
1 tsp harissa paste
Juice of ½ lemon
A handful of fresh cilantro

Serves 2

Heat the olive oil in a large heavy-bottomed saucepan. Add the onion, leeks, carrots, celery, and potato and cook gently for about 10 minutes or until the vegetables have softened but not colored.

Add the lentils and harissa. Pour in the stock and bring to a boil. Simmer, partially covered, for a further 25 minutes until the vegetables and lentils are tender.

Add the lemon juice, season to taste with a little salt and black pepper, and stir in the fresh cilantro.

NUTRITION per serving:
• 279 cals • 11 g protein • 7 g fat (1 g saturates)
• 37 g carbs (9 g total sugars) • 11 g fiber

CARROT SOUP WITH QUINOA

This simple soup is full of beta-carotene, which is good for the immune system and for promoting recovery after exercise. It's made extra nutritious by the addition of quinoa, which adds not only interesting texture but also extra protein and iron.

1 tbsp light olive or rapeseed oil
1 onion, finely chopped
1 garlic clove, crushed
3 carrots, sliced
2 cups vegetable stock
(2 tsp vegetable bouillon)
1 bay leaf
¼ cup quinoa
A handful of flat leaf parsley, roughly chopped

Serves 2

Heat the oil in a large saucepan over medium heat, add the onion and garlic, and fry for 2–3 min.

Add the carrots to the pan and mix well. Cook gently over moderately low heat for 5 minutes, stirring occasionally, until the vegetables soften a little. Add the stock and bay leaf and bring to a boil. Simmer for 15 minutes or until the vegetables are tender. Remove and discard the bay leaf. Purée the soup using a hand blender or conventional blender.

Meanwhile cook the quinoa according to the pack instructions. Ladle the soup into bowls, then top with the quinoa and fresh parsley.

NUTRITION per serving:
• 223 cals • 6 g protein • 8 g fat (1 g saturates)
• 30 g carbs (15 g total sugars) • 7 g fiber

BUTTERNUT SQUASH SOUP
WITH CANNELLINI BEANS

Butternut squash has a beautiful, sweet flavor, which is really brought out by the addition of ginger and nutmeg. It is, of course, also packed with antioxidant carotenoids, which boost the immune system and protect cells from damaging free radicals. I've added canned cannellini beans to boost the protein content of the soup.

1 tbsp light olive or rapeseed oil

1 small onion, chopped

¼ medium butternut squash, peeled and cut into chunks

1 carrot, sliced

1 garlic clove, crushed

½ tsp fresh ginger, grated

Pinch of nutmeg, freshly grated (optional)

2 cups vegetable stock (2 tsp vegetable bouillon)

½ (14 oz) can cannellini beans, drained and rinsed

Salt and freshly ground black pepper

Optional: Greek yogurt, wholegrain toast

Serves 2

Heat the oil in a large saucepan over moderate heat. Add the onion and cook gently for about 5 minutes until softened. Add the butternut squash, carrot, garlic, ginger, and optional nutmeg. Stir and continue cooking for a few minutes. Add the vegetable stock, bring to a boil, lower the heat, cover, and simmer for about 20 minutes until the vegetables are tender.

Remove from the heat and blend until smooth using a blender, food processor, or a hand blender.

Return to the saucepan, add the cannellini beans, and heat through again. Season with salt and freshly ground black pepper. Serve with a dollop of Greek yogurt if desired and a couple of slices of wholegrain toast.

NUTRITION per serving:
• 187 cals • 7 g protein • 6 g fat (1 g saturates)
• 21 g carbs (9 g total sugars) • 9 g fiber

PUMPKIN SOUP

It's healthy, satisfying, and comforting—I must confess to a weakness for pumpkin soup in the autumn months when pumpkins are in season. Pumpkins are super-rich in the phytonutrient alpha-carotene, which helps protect against cell damage. They also supply vitamin E, beta-carotene, and vitamin C. This soup is perfect as a pre- or post-workout meal served with hummus (see page 191) and toast.

1 tbsp light olive or rapeseed oil

1 onion, chopped

½ in fresh ginger, grated

1 garlic clove, crushed

½ tsp grated nutmeg

½ tsp ground coriander

1 carrot, sliced

1 small potato, peeled and chopped

1 ½ cups pumpkin flesh, chopped

2 cups vegetable stock

Salt and freshly ground black pepper

2 tbsp pumpkin seeds, toasted

Optional: Pita bread, hummus, for serving

Serves 2

Heat the olive oil in a large saucepan, add the onion, and sauté over moderate heat for about 5 minutes until it is translucent. Add the ginger, garlic, nutmeg, and coriander and cook for a further minute.

Add the prepared vegetables, stir well, cover, and continue cooking gently for a further 5 minutes. Add the stock, bring to a boil, reduce the heat, and simmer for about 20 minutes or until the vegetables are tender.

Purée the soup using a hand blender or conventional blender. Add a little more water or stock if you want a thinner consistency. Season to taste, ladle into bowls, and scatter the pumpkin seeds on top. Serve with toasted pita bread and hummus.

> **NUTRITION per serving:**
> • 260 cals • 8 g protein • 13 g fat (2 g saturates)
> • 23 g carbs (10 g total sugars) • 8 g fiber

HOW TO TOAST PUMPKIN SEEDS

Arrange the seeds in an even layer on a baking tray and place in the oven at 350 °F for 12–15 minutes until they are fragrant and toasted.
Check them often and stir halfway through the cooking time to make sure they do not burn.

SPINACH AND ZUCCHINI SOUP WITH TOASTED ALMONDS

This healthy soup is full of green goodness, easy to make, and a brilliant way of getting your daily iron. You can swap the spinach for other green veg in season, such as savoy cabbage, kale, or spring greens. I've added chickpeas for extra protein and thickness.

1 tbsp light olive or rapeseed oil
1 small onion, finely chopped
4 cups fresh or frozen spinach
1 zucchini, sliced
2 cups vegetable stock
½ (14 oz) can chickpeas, drained
Salt and freshly ground black pepper
A little nutmeg, freshly grated
A squeeze of lemon juice
⅓ cup sliced almonds, toasted under the grill
Optional: Wholegrain bread, for serving
Serves 2

Heat the olive oil in a heavy-bottomed saucepan over moderate heat and cook the onion for 5 minutes. Then add the spinach, zucchini, and vegetable stock, bring to a boil, cover, and simmer for a further 4–5 minutes until the vegetables are tender.

Put the soup onto a blender with the chickpeas, salt, pepper, nutmeg, and lemon juice and blend until smooth. Warm through, then ladle the soup into bowls and sprinkle the sliced almonds over the top. Serve with wholegrain bread.

NUTRITION per serving:
• 267 cals • 12 g protein • 15 g fat (2 g saturates)
• 17 g carbs (5 g total sugars) • 10 g fiber

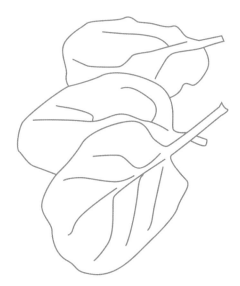

SERIOUSLY GREEN SOUP

This super-healthy soup is loaded with nutritious green vegetables such as broccoli, cabbage, and kale. It's packed with flavor and is a great way of getting your daily dose of vitamins and minerals.

1 tbsp light olive or rapeseed oil

1 onion, finely sliced

2 garlic cloves, crushed

1 leek, sliced

1 ½ cups broccoli florets

2 cups Savoy cabbage, spring greens, kale, or chard, finely shredded

1 small potato, peeled and diced

2 cups vegetable stock

Freshly ground black pepper

A handful fresh cilantro

Optional: Seeded bread, for serving

Serves 2

Heat the olive oil in a heavy-bottomed saucepan over moderate heat. Add the onion, garlic, and leek and cook gently for about 5 minutes.

Add the remaining vegetables to the pan and mix well. Cook over moderately low heat for a few minutes, stirring occasionally, then add the stock. Bring to a boil then simmer for 15 minutes or until the vegetables are tender. Add the cilantro, season with black pepper, and purée in a blender.

Serve with seeded bread.

NUTRITION per serving:
- 210 cals • 8 g protein • 7 g fat (1 g saturates)
- 23 g carbs (8 g total sugars) • 11 g fiber

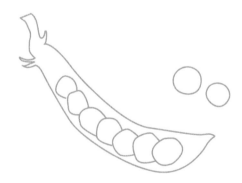

ROOT VEGETABLE SOUP

This is one of my favorite soups, mainly because of its simplicity but also because it's so full of winter flavors! You can experiment with different root veg—celeriac and sweet potatoes also work well—or add spices such as chili, cumin, cinnamon, or coriander for a spicier soup.

1 tbsp light olive or rapeseed oil

1 onion, finely sliced

2 carrots, sliced

1 parsnip, diced

1 ½ cups rutabaga, diced

2 cups vegetable stock

1 bay leaf

Salt and freshly ground black pepper

Optional: Greek yogurt, wholegrain rolls

Serves 2

Heat the olive oil in a heavy-bottomed saucepan over moderate heat. Add the onion and sauté gently for about 5 minutes until it is translucent.

Add the carrots, parsnips, and rutabaga to the pan and mix well. Cook gently over moderately low heat for 5 minutes, stirring occasionally, until the vegetables soften a little.

Add the stock and bay leaf and bring to a boil. Simmer for 15 minutes or until the vegetables are tender.

Allow the soup to cool slightly for a couple of minutes. Remove and discard the bay leaf. Purée the soup using a hand blender or conventional blender. Season to taste with salt and pepper. Serve with a dollop of Greek yogurt (if desired) and crusty wholegrain rolls.

NUTRITION per serving:
• 181 cals • 3 g protein • 7 g fat (1 g saturates)
• 21 g carbs (15 g total sugars) • 10 g fiber

ROASTED MEDITERRANEAN VEGETABLE SOUP

VG

Bursting with flavor and full of fresh vegetables, this soup is a great way of boosting your vitamin C intake. The vegetables are roasted in the oven to bring out their natural sweetness and then simmered in stock. If you prefer a smooth soup, blend it in a blender.

1 tbsp light olive or rapeseed oil
1 small onion, thinly sliced
2 garlic cloves, finely chopped
½ red and ½ green pepper, sliced
1 zucchini, trimmed and sliced
1 cup tomatoes, diced
¼ eggplant, diced
2 cups vegetable stock
(2 tsp vegetable bouillon)
Salt and freshly ground black pepper
2 tsp pesto
Optional: Wholegrain bread w/ricotta, for serving

Serves 2

Preheat the oven to 400 °F.

Place all the vegetables in a roasting pan. Drizzle the olive oil on top and toss lightly so that the vegetables are well coated. Roast in the oven for about 30 minutes until the vegetables are slightly charred on the outside and tender in the middle.

Put half the veg in a blender along with half the stock and process until smooth.

Bring the remaining stock to a boil in a saucepan, then add the puréed veg and the remaining roasted veg. Heat through and season to taste with salt and freshly ground black pepper.

Ladle into bowls, adding a teaspoon of pesto to each bowl immediately before serving, and serve with a couple of slices of wholegrain bread spread with ricotta.

NUTRITION per serving:
• 188 cals • 6 g protein • 9 g fat (1 g saturates)
• 16 g carbs (13 g total sugars) • 9 g fiber

RED LENTIL AND VEGETABLE SOUP

Lentil soup is comforting, simple, and easy to make with the bare minimum of ingredients. Red lentils are filling and highly nutritious, packed with fiber, protein, vitamins, and minerals, and provide a sustained energy release. This soup makes a great pre-workout meal.

1 tbsp light olive or rapeseed oil

1 onion, chopped

1–2 garlic cloves, crushed

1 carrot, sliced

⅓ cup red lentils

2 cups vegetable stock
(2 tsp vegetable bouillon)

Salt and freshly ground black pepper, to taste

Juice of ½ lemon

Optional: Yogurt, veg parmesan, crusty bread, for serving

Serves 2

Heat the oil in a large saucepan. Add the onion and cook over moderate heat for about 5 minutes until soft, stirring occasionally. Stir in the garlic and cook for 1 minute, stirring continuously. Add the carrots, lentils, and stock. Bring to a boil and skim off any scum that appears on the surface. Reduce the heat and simmer for about 20–25 minutes until the lentils begin to fall apart.

Season with salt and black pepper and thin with a little water if necessary. Season and add the lemon juice before serving. Serve with a dollop of yogurt or grated vegetarian Parmesan (if desired) and some crusty bread.

NUTRITION per serving:
• 229 cals • 11 g protein • 7 g fat (1 g saturates)
• 29 g carbs (7 g total sugars) • 7 g fiber

CHAPTER 5

SALADS

Clockwise from right: *Goat cheese and avocado salad,*
Halloumi and red pepper salad, Rainbow salad with goats' cheese

QUINOA SALAD WITH ROASTED MEDITERRANEAN VEGETABLES

This nutritious salad is full of amazing Mediterranean flavors. It's my favorite combination of vegetables but feel free to substitute with any other veg you have on hand, such as butternut squash or carrots. The resulting dish will be full of valuable phytonutrients, vitamin C, beta-carotene, and fiber.

$1/2$ red pepper, thickly sliced
1 zucchini, thickly sliced
1 small red onion, roughly sliced
$1/2$ eggplant, cut into 1-in cubes
A handful of cherry tomatoes
A few sprigs of rosemary
1 garlic clove, crushed
2–3 tbsp olive oil
$2/3$ cup quinoa
$1 1/4$ cups vegetable stock or water
1 tbsp lemon juice
$1/2$ cup feta, crumbled
A small handful of basil or mint leaves

Serves 2

Preheat the oven to 400 °F.

Place all the vegetables in a large roasting pan. Place the rosemary sprigs between the vegetables and scatter over the crushed garlic. Drizzle half the olive oil on top, and toss lightly so that the vegetables are well coated. Roast in the oven for about 30 minutes until the vegetables are slightly charred on the outside and tender in the middle.

Meanwhile cook the quinoa. Place in a saucepan with the stock or water, bring to a boil, lower the heat, then simmer for about 15–20 minutes until the water has been absorbed.

To make the dressing, combine the rest of the oil and lemon juice in a screw-top jar and shake until combined. Add to the quinoa, roasted vegetables, and crumbled feta.

NUTRITION per serving:
• 436 cals • 16 g protein • 20 g fat (6 g saturates)
• 44 g carbs (13 g total sugars) • 6 g fiber

CHICKPEA SALAD WITH WATERCRESS AND CASHEWS

Chickpeas make a nutritious and filling base for a salad. They are rich in protein, fiber, and fructo-oligosachharides (a type of fiber that increases the friendly bacteria in the gut). I've combined them with cashews, watercress, and fresh cilantro, all of which provide extra iron and add a lovely contrast of textures and colors.

2 cups green beans, trimmed
1 (14 oz) can chickpeas, drained and rinsed
$^1/_3$ cup cashews, lightly toasted
A small handful of fresh cilantro, chopped
1 $^1/_4$ cups watercress

For the dressing:
2 tbsp extra virgin olive oil
1 tbsp balsamic vinegar
1 garlic clove, crushed
$^1/_2$ tsp Dijon mustard

Serves 2

Steam the beans for 4 minutes until they are tender-crisp. Drain, then refresh under cold running water.

Place in a large bowl and combine with the chickpeas, cashews, and cilantro.

Place the dressing ingredients in a bottle or screw-top jar and shake until combined. Add half of the dressing to the chickpea salad and mix until well combined.

Place the watercress in a bowl and toss with the remaining dressing. Pile the chickpea salad on the watercress.

NUTRITION per serving:
• 439 cals • 17 g protein • 38 g fat (5 g saturates)
• 26 g carbs (3 g total sugars) • 11 g fiber

RAINBOW SALAD WITH GOAT CHEESE

Here's a brilliant way of getting your 5-a-day all in one meal. It's literally a rainbow of colourful vegetables and packed full of phytonutrients. Some of the veg are raw, so all their vitamin C is intact; some are cooked in olive oil, which enhances the absorption of beta-carotene and vitamin E. I add avocado for its heart-healthy monounsaturated fat and goat cheese for its high protein content, but you can substitute feta or cottage cheese if you prefer.

1 tbsp olive oil

1–2 garlic cloves, crushed

1 red pepper, sliced

1/2 red onion, sliced

1/4 butternut squash, peeled and cubed

1 carrot, cut into batons

1 sweet potato, peeled and cubed

2 handfuls of salad leaves, e.g. baby spinach, arugula, and watercress

A handful of cherry tomatoes

1/2 avocado, sliced

1/2 cup goat cheese

Serves 2

Preheat the oven to 400 °F.

Toss the pepper, onion, butternut squash, carrot, and sweet potato in the olive oil and garlic in a large roasting pan. Roast in the oven for about 30 minutes until the vegetables are almost tender.

Arrange the salad leaves, tomatoes, and avocado on two plates. Pile the cooked vegetables and top with crumbled goat cheese.

NUTRITION per serving:
• 520 cals • 18 g protein • 30 g fat (14 g saturates)
• 40 g carbs (21 g total sugars) • 11 g fiber

HALLOUMI AND RED PEPPER SALAD

This is my go-to salad in the summer months—all the delicious fresh vegetables in this salad conjure up thoughts of holidays in the Med. Peppers and tomatoes are excellent sources of vitamin C and phytonutrients. Halloumi is slightly lower in fat than most hard cheeses. When it's grilled, barbecued, or fried it becomes beautifully crispy and savory on the outside. Avocado and pine nuts both provide healthy monounsaturated fats and vitamin E.

¹/₄ lb (4 oz) halloumi

2 tbsp pine nuts, toasted

2 large handfuls of salad leaves e.g. baby spinach, arugula, and watercress

1 red pepper, sliced

5-6 cherry tomatoes, halved

1 avocado, sliced

1 tbsp extra virgin olive oil

A squeeze of lemon juice

Salt and freshly ground black pepper

Serves 2

Heat a griddle or frying pan over high heat. Cut the halloumi into ¼-in-thick slices and fry for 1–1½ minutes on each side until golden. Set aside.

Toast the pine nuts in the dry frying pan.

Arrange the salad leaves on two plates. Scatter the peppers, tomatoes, and avocado slices on top. Arrange the halloumi slices on top.

Whisk together the oil, lemon juice, and seasoning. Drizzle over the salad and scatter the pine nuts on top.

NUTRITION per serving:
- 559 cals • 19 g protein • 47 g fat (15 g saturates)
- 11 g carbs (8 g total sugars) • 8 g fiber

TOFU AND SPINACH SALAD WITH TOASTED ALMONDS

This super-quick salad makes a perfect lunch served with a little coarse-grain bread.

2 handfuls of baby spinach leaves
1 small red onion, thinly sliced
1 orange, peeled and thinly sliced
1 tbsp extra virgin olive oil
1 tsp lemon juice
1 tsp wholegrain mustard
7 oz smoked tofu, diced
Freshly ground black pepper
¼ cup sliced almonds, toasted
Optional: Seeded bread, for serving
Serves 2

Place the spinach leaves in a large salad bowl. Add the onion and orange slices.

Place the extra virgin olive oil, lemon juice, and mustard in a bottle or screw-top jar and shake thoroughly. Pour over the salad leaves then toss to combine.

Arrange the tofu on top of the salad, grind over some black pepper, then scatter the almonds on top. Serve with seeded bread.

> NUTRITION per serving:
> • 391 cals • 21 g protein • 26 g fat (2 g saturates)
> • 14 g carbs (11 g total sugars) • 8 g fiber

TABBOULEH

This wonderfully fragrant summer salad is made with whole grains of cracked wheat, fresh herbs, and lycopene-rich tomatoes. Bulgur wheat is rich in fiber, iron, zinc, selenium, and vitamin E. The tomatoes in this salad add cancer-protective lycopene, and both tomatoes and green pepper provide extra vitamin C.

⅔ cup bulgur wheat
Salt and freshly ground black pepper
4 spring onions, finely chopped
1 tbsp extra virgin olive oil
Juice of ½ lemon
½ red or green bell pepper, finely chopped
A handful of flat leaf parsley, chopped
A handful of mint leaves, chopped
3–4 small tomatoes, chopped
Optional: Crumbled feta, toasted nuts
Serves 2

Place the bulgur wheat in a bowl and add hot water until just covered. Leave for 15 minutes, drain, then transfer back to the bowl. Season with salt and freshly ground black pepper.

Add the spring onions, olive oil, lemon juice, green pepper, parsley, mint, and tomatoes and combine all the ingredients. Place in the fridge for at least 30 minutes to allow the flavors to infuse.

Serve with crumbled feta cheese or a handful of toasted nuts.

> NUTRITION per serving:
> • 303 cals • 8 g protein • 7 g fat (1 g saturates)
> • 50 g carbs (4 g total sugars) • 7 g fiber

QUINOA AND RED KIDNEY BEAN SALAD

This tasty combination of quinoa and beans has a low glycemic index and provides an excellent balance of protein and complex carbohydrates—perfect before a long workout or for refueling afterwards. I like to add almonds for extra crunch—as well as protein and calcium—but feel free to substitute other varieties of nuts or seeds.

2/3 cup quinoa

1 1/4 cups water or vegetable stock

1 (14 oz) can red kidney beans, drained and rinsed

4 spring onions, chopped

A handful of plum cherry tomatoes, halved

1/4 cup toasted sliced almonds

For the dressing:

2 tbsp extra virgin olive oil

2 tsp lemon juice

1/2 tsp runny honey (optional)

Salt and freshly ground black pepper

Serves 2

Place the quinoa in a pan with the water or stock. Bring to a boil, then lower the heat, cover, and simmer for about 20 minutes until the quinoa is tender. Remove from the heat, drain if necessary, and transfer to a bowl.

Add the beans, spring onions, tomatoes, and almonds and mix to combine.

To make the dressing, place the olive oil, lemon juice, honey (if desired), salt, and pepper in a screw-top glass jar and shake well until mixed. Pour the dressing over the salad and toss well until all the ingredients are coated in the dressing. Serve with a green salad.

NUTRITION per serving:
• 543 cals • 22 g protein • 22 g fat (3 g saturates)
• 59 g carbs (12 g total sugars) • 13 g fiber

HOW TO TOAST ALMONDS

1 Place in a nonstick frying pan over a medium heat, stirring frequently until they turn golden brown. OR

2 Preheat the oven to 350 °F. Spread the nuts in a single layer on a baking sheet and bake for 10–15 minutes, stirring occasionally, until golden.

CHICKPEA AND ROASTED PEPPER SALAD ⓋⒼ
WITH WALNUTS

I love the contrasting textures, colors, and flavors in this salad. It's super-healthy too—providing plenty of protein, carbohydrates, and fiber. It's also packed with recovery-boosting omega-3s from the walnuts, vitamin C, iron, and phytonutrients.

$^1/_2$ red onion, cut into wedges

$^1/_2$ red pepper, cut into wedges

1 garlic clove, crushed

1 tbsp olive oil

1 (14 oz) can chickpeas, drained and rinsed

1 $^1/_4$ cups watercress

$^1/_2$ cup walnuts, lightly toasted

For the dressing:

1 tbsp extra virgin olive oil

2 tsp balsamic vinegar

1 garlic clove, crushed

½ tsp Dijon mustard

Optional: Crusty bread, cottage cheese or goat cheese

Serves 2

Preheat the oven to 400 °F.

Toss the peppers, red onion, and garlic together in a baking tray with 1 tbsp olive oil and roast for 20–25 minutes until the edges begin to turn brown.

Place the dressing ingredients in a screw-top glass jar and shake until combined. Mix together the chickpeas, roasted vegetables, and dressing.

Arrange the watercress on two plates. Top with the chickpea salad and scatter the toasted walnuts.

Serve with crusty bread after a long endurance workout, or some cottage cheese or goat cheese after a tough strength and conditioning session.

> **NUTRITION per serving:**
> • 482 cals • 16 g protein • 33 g fat (4 g saturates)
> • 26 g carbs (6 g total sugars) • 11 g fiber

HOW TO TOAST WALNUTS

1 Place in a nonstick frying pan over a medium heat, stirring frequently until they turn golden brown. OR

2 Preheat the oven to 350 °F. Spread the nuts in a single layer on a baking tray and bake for 8–12 minutes, stirring occasionally, until lightly toasted.

WARM LENTIL SALAD WITH BABY SPINACH AND WALNUTS

Lentils are a brilliant way of getting your daily iron quota. Try to combine them with other ingredients rich in vitamin C, as this will increase iron uptake by the body. Here they are paired with tomatoes and spinach, both of which are good sources of vitamin C. The walnuts add extra protein, along with omega-3 fats and zinc. I like it warm, but it's equally good when eaten cold.

1 ¼ cups ready-prepared lentils*
(I use Merchant Gourmet)

4 spring onions, finely chopped

4–5 cherry tomatoes, halved

½ cup walnut pieces

A small handful of mint leaves, roughly chopped

Low-sodium salt and freshly ground black pepper

2 handfuls of baby spinach leaves

For the dressing:

Juice of ½ lime

2 tbsp extra virgin olive oil

1 tbsp wine vinegar

*Alternatively, you can use canned lentils or ½ cup dried lentils, soaked and boiled for 30 minutes

Serves 2

Put the lentils in a saucepan with 2 tablespoons water and warm through for a few minutes. Drain and transfer to a bowl. Mix with the spring onions, tomatoes, walnuts, and chopped mint.

Place the lime juice, olive oil, and vinegar in a screw-top jar and shake well. Pour the dressing over the warm lentils. Toss lightly and season with low-sodium salt and pepper.

Arrange the baby spinach leaves on a serving plate and pile the lentil salad on top.

> NUTRITION per serving:
> • 491 cals • 20 g protein • 30 g fat (4 g saturates)
> • 30 g carbs (5 g total sugars) • 11 g fiber

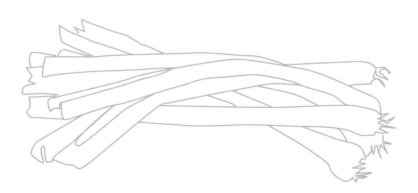

GOAT CHEESE AND AVOCADO SALAD WITH WALNUTS

This is my favorite summer salad—and super easy to assemble. It's full of healthy monounsaturated fats and recovery-boosting omega-3s, courtesy of the avocado and walnuts. I love the mild, crumbly texture of young, firm goat cheese with a soft white coat (such as Capricorn) but you can use other varieties of cheese if you prefer.

1 romaine lettuce head, tough outer leaves removed
1 red pepper, sliced
1 carrot, grated
½ small cucumber, sliced
2 tomatoes, quartered
1 ripe avocado
Salt and freshly ground black pepper, to taste
1 cup goat cheese, crumbled
¹/₂ cup walnuts, chopped

For the dressing:
1 tbsp lime or lemon juice
1 garlic clove, crushed
2 tbsp extra virgin olive oil
Serves 2

Cut the lettuce leaves into ½-in pieces and place them in a large bowl. Add the peppers, carrots, cucumber, and tomatoes. Halve, peel, and pit the avocados. Cut them into ¼-in dice and add to the other vegetables.

Place the dressing ingredients in a screw-top jar and shake well. Pour over the salad and toss well. Top with the goat cheese and chopped walnuts.

NUTRITION per serving:
- 505 cals • 15 g protein • 40 g fat (14 g saturates)
- 16 g carbs (15 g total sugars) • 10 g fiber

CHAPTER 6

MAIN MEALS

· ·

Potato, spinach and goat cheese frittata

SPICY CHICKPEA AND SPINACH STEW

When it starts to get chilly, this is the perfect recipe for a warming mid-week meal. Chickpeas are an excellent source of fiber, protein, and iron. They also contain fructo-oligosaccharides, a type of fiber that increases the friendly bacteria of the gut. Here, I've combined them with spinach, which is a fantastic source of folate and iron.

1 tbsp light olive oil or rapeseed oil

1 small onion, chopped

1–2 garlic cloves, crushed

$^1/_3$ inch fresh ginger, peeled and finely grated

$^1/_2$ green chili, finely chopped

$^1/_2$ tsp ground coriander

$^1/_2$ tsp ground cumin

$^1/_4$ tsp turmeric

$^1/_2$ (14 oz) can chopped tomatoes

1 (14 oz) can chickpeas, drained and rinsed

2 cups baby spinach

Salt and freshly ground black pepper

A handful of fresh cilantro leaves, chopped

Optional: 2 tbsp low-fat plain Greek yogurt, wholegrain couscous, wholegrain rice

Serves 2

Heat the oil in a large heavy-bottomed saucepan and add the onion, garlic, ginger, chili, coriander, cumin, and turmeric. Cook over moderate heat for 10 minutes until the onions have softened.

Add the tomatoes and chickpeas. Bring to a boil, then simmer for 10 minutes. Add the spinach and stir until the spinach has wilted. Remove from the heat, season with salt and pepper, and stir in the fresh cilantro.

Serve with the Greek yogurt (if desired), and wholegrain couscous or wholegrain rice.

> **NUTRITION per serving:**
> • 294 cals • 18 g protein • 10 g fat (1 g saturates)
> • 29 g carbs (9 g total sugars) • 10 g fiber

BUTTER BEANS WITH BUTTERNUT SQUASH VG AND SPINACH

This stew is perfect on a cold night in, warming and super tasty. Butter beans are a fantastic source of protein as well as fiber, iron, and zinc. Here, they are teamed with spinach for extra iron, folic acid, and vitamin C, and butternut squash, which supplies beta-carotene.

1 tbsp light olive oil or rapeseed oil

1 small onion, chopped

1–2 garlic cloves, crushed

½ medium butternut squash, peeled and chopped

½ (14 oz) can chopped tomatoes

½ cup vegetable stock

½ tsp dried thyme

1 (14 oz) can butter beans, drained and rinsed

2 cups baby spinach

Salt and freshly ground black pepper

A small handful fresh cilantro, chopped

Optional: Baked potatoes and green vegetables, grated cheese, for serving

Serves 2

Heat the oil in a nonstick heavy-bottomed pan, add the onion, and cook over a moderate heat for 5 minutes.

Add the garlic, butternut squash, chopped tomatoes, vegetable stock, thyme, and butter beans. Stir, then bring to a boil.
Lower the heat and simmer for 20 minutes, stirring occasionally.
Stir in the spinach, turn off the heat, cover, and leave for 2 minutes.
Season and stir in the fresh cilantro.

Scatter grated cheese on top if desired, and serve with baked potatoes and a green vegetable, such as broccoli or green beans.

NUTRITION per serving:
• 283 cals • 15 g protein • 7 g fat (1 g saturates)
• 33 g carbs (12 g total sugars) • 15 g fiber

CHICKPEA BURGERS

These protein-packed burgers are a delicious alternative to shop-bought veggie burgers. Made mostly from store cupboard standbys, they are also rich in beta-carotene and fiber, and take only 10 minutes to prepare. I like to add cumin, coriander, and paprika, but feel free to experiment with a different combination of spices and flavors.

1 (14 oz) can chickpeas, drained

⅓ cup old-fashioned rolled oats

2 carrots, roughly chopped

½ tsp each: ground cumin, ground coriander, and paprika

Salt and freshly ground black pepper

Small handful of chopped fresh cilantro

1 egg

2 tbsp each: sunflower seeds and pumpkin seeds

Olive oil, for brushing

Optional: Baked sweet potatoes, leafy salad, low-fat plain Greek yogurt, for serving

Makes 8

Preheat the oven to 375 °F.

Place all the ingredients except the egg and seeds in a food processor and process for about 30 seconds until thoroughly combined. You may need to stop to scrape down the bowl during the process. Add the egg and process for a further 10–15 seconds.

Transfer the mixture to a large bowl and stir in the sunflower and pumpkin seeds. Shape the mixture into 8 patties and place on an oiled baking tray. Brush the burgers with a little olive oil. Bake in the oven for 25–30 minutes until they are crisp and golden.

Serve with a baked sweet potato (or in a wholegrain bun) with spinach or a leafy salad and a generous dollop of low-fat plain Greek yogurt.

NUTRITION per burger:
• 127 cals • 6 g protein • 6 g fat (1 g saturates)
• (2 g total sugars) • 4 g fiber

BLACK BEAN AND VEGETABLE CURRY WITH ALMONDS

This protein-packed curry is delicious and really easy to make. Black beans are rich in protein as well as fiber and iron. Both the yogurt and almonds supply useful amounts of calcium. Make a larger quantity and keep the remaining portions in the fridge for up to 3 days or freeze for up to 3 months.

1 tbsp light olive oil or rapeseed oil

1 onion, chopped

1 carrot, sliced

1 medium potato, peeled and cut into cubes

¹/₂ butternut squash, peeled and cut into cubes

1 ¹/₂ cups broccoli florets

¹/₃ cup frozen peas

¹/₂ tsp of each: cumin, coriander, and turmeric

1 garlic clove, crushed

1 tsp grated fresh ginger

¹/₂ (14 oz) can chopped tomatoes

1 (14 oz) can black beans, drained and rinsed

¹/₄ cup coconut milk

¹/₄ cup low-fat plain Greek yogurt

¹/₄ cup ground almonds

Small handful fresh cilantro leaves, chopped

Salt and freshly ground black pepper

Optional: Chapatis or flatbread, for serving

Serves 2

Heat the oil in a large pan and add the onion. Cook gently for 5 minutes until softened. Add the vegetables, spices, garlic, and ginger and cook for a further minute, then add the chopped tomatoes and about ½ cup water. Bring to a boil, turn down the heat, and cook for 10 minutes. Add the beans and continue cooking for 2–3 minutes.

In a separate bowl, mix together the coconut milk, yogurt, and almonds, then stir into the curry. Turn off the heat, taking care not to boil, otherwise the yogurt may curdle. Stir in the cilantro and season with salt and freshly ground black pepper.

Serve with wholegrain rice or wholegrain chapatis or flatbreads.

NUTRITION per serving:
- 592 cals • 26 g protein • 21 g fat (7 g saturates)
- 66 g carbs (22 g total sugars) • 18 g fiber

LENTIL AND RICE PILAF

This is one of my all-time favorite pre-workout meals. The combination of brown basmati rice and lentils produces sustained energy and wards off hunger. Brown lentils are particularly rich in protein, iron, and fiber. Tuscan kale and broccoli add extra iron, folate, and vitamin C, making this a truly nutrient-packed dish.

1 tbsp light olive or rapeseed oil
1 small onion, chopped
1–2 garlic cloves, crushed
¾ cup brown basmati rice
½ cup + 2 tbsp brown lentils (dried)
2 cups (1 pint) vegetable stock
1 cup kale or Tuscan kale, shredded
1 cup broccoli florets
¾ cup green beans, trimmed and cut into 1-in lengths
⅓ cup frozen peas
1 tsp dried Herbes de Provence (or mixed herbs)
3 tbsp cashews
Optional: A little grated Parmesan, salt and freshly ground black pepper
Serves 2

Heat the oil in a large nonstick pan and cook the onion for 3–4 minutes. Add the garlic and cook a further minute. Add the basmati rice, lentils, and the vegetable stock, bring to a boil, then simmer for 20–25 minutes. Make sure it does not boil dry; add extra stock if necessary.

Add the vegetables and herbs and continue cooking over a gentle heat for a further 7 minutes. Stir in the cashews, season with salt and pepper, and serve with a little grated parmesan if you wish.

NUTRITION per serving:
• 647 cals • 28 g protein • 16 g fat (3 g saturates)
• 89 g carbs (7 g total sugars) • 17 g fiber

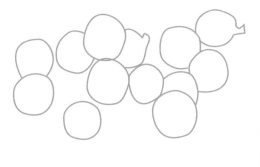

QUINOA, CHICKPEA, AND SPINACH STEW

This is one of my favorite ways of cooking quinoa. It's very easy to make as everything is cooked in one pan. Quinoa contains 1½ times more protein than most grains, twice as much iron, as well as magnesium, calcium, and B vitamins. The dish is high in protein, but the addition of apricots, spinach, almonds, and pumpkin seeds also make this dish a fantastic source of iron—and the peppers and spinach provide vitamin C to aid iron absorption by the body.

1 tbsp light olive oil or rapeseed oil
1 small onion, chopped
A pinch of ground cinnamon
3–4 cardamom pods
2 garlic cloves, crushed
½ yellow pepper, chopped
1 leek, cleaned and chopped
²/₃ cup quinoa (dry)
1 ¼ cups vegetable stock or water
1 (14 oz) can chickpeas, drained
¼ cup ready-to-eat dried apricots
2 handfuls baby spinach leaves
¼ cup toasted sliced almonds
¼ cup toasted pumpkin seeds

Serves 2

Heat the olive oil in a large nonstick pan and cook the onion for 3–4 minutes. Add the cinnamon, cardamom, and garlic and cook for a further 2 minutes. Add the pepper and leek and continue cooking for 2 minutes more.

Add the quinoa, stock, chickpeas, and apricots. Stir and bring to a boil. Reduce the heat and simmer for about 20 minutes until the liquid has absorbed and the quinoa is cooked. Stir in the spinach and turn off the heat. It will cook in the heat of the pan.

Stir in the almonds and pumpkin seeds.

NUTRITION per serving:
• 646 cals • 28 g protein • 26 g fat (3 g saturates)
• 68 g carbs (16 g total sugars) • 14 g fiber

WHAT IS QUINOA?

A "pseudograin," quinoa (pronounced "keen-wah") is mild and slightly nutty, with a similar texture to couscous. Technically quinoa is not a true grain, but is the seed of the Chenopodium or Goosefoot plant. It is used as a grain and substituted for grains because of its cooking characteristics. Beets, spinach, and Swiss chard are all relatives of quinoa. It is high in protein, calcium, and iron, and is a relatively good source of vitamin E and several of the B vitamins. It contains all nine essential amino acids and is exceptionally high in lysine, cysteine, and methionine-amino acids, typically low in other grains. It is a good complement to beans and lentils, which are often low in methionine and cysteine.

BLACK BEAN TACOS WITH SALSA

Tacos are a great sharing food, so this recipe works equally well as a family dish or as a speedy meal for two. Black beans are super-nutritious, full of protein, iron, and fiber, while the raw salsa is packed with vitamin C and antioxidants. Any leftover salsa can be kept in the fridge for up to 3 days.

4 corn tacos

1 (14 oz) can black beans, drained

2 tsp olive oil

½ tsp ground cumin

½ tsp paprika

¼ tsp ground coriander

For the salsa:

1 large ripe tomato, skinned, deseeded, and finely diced

1 tbsp fresh cilantro, chopped

½ tsp finely chopped fresh chili (or according to your taste)

1 small clove of garlic, crushed

1 tsp olive oil

¼ red onion, finely chopped

1 tbsp lemon or lime juice

Optional: 2 tbsp low-fat plain Greek yogurt, for serving

Leafy salad and cooked rice, for serving

Serves 2

In a bowl, mix together the black beans, olive oil, cumin, paprika, and coriander.

In a separate bowl, make the salsa by combining all the ingredients together.

Warm the taco shells according to pack instructions. Take the tacos, bean mixture, salsa, and yogurt (if desired) to the table in separate bowls and let everyone serve themselves. Serve with a leafy salad and cooked rice.

NUTRITION per serving:
- 290 cals • 18 g protein • 13 g fat (1 g saturates)
- 21 g carbs (7 g total sugars) • 10 g fiber

DHAL WITH BUTTERNUT SQUASH AND SPINACH

Lentils provide an excellent balance of protein and carbohydrate, along with lots of fiber and iron. A dhal is a really speedy dish and, with extra vegetables such as butternut squash and spinach, a brilliant way of getting extra vitamins and minerals. You can add other veg that you have handy—leeks, cauliflower, zucchini, or sweet potatoes also work well.

1 small onion, chopped

1 tbsp olive oil or rapeseed oil

1 garlic clove, crushed

$^1/_2$ tsp ground cumin

1 tsp ground coriander

$^1/_2$ tsp turmeric

$^1/_2$ cup + 2 tbsp red lentils

½ small butternut squash, peeled and diced

1 cup spinach

$^1/_4$ cup cashews, toasted

Juice of $^1/_2$ lemon

Salt to season

Small handful of fresh cilantro, finely chopped

Optional: Cooked wholegrain rice or wholegrain chapati, for serving

Serves 2

Heat the oil in a heavy-bottomed pan and sauté the onions for 5 minutes. Add the garlic and spices and continue cooking for another minute, stirring continuously.

Add the lentils and cover with enough water to come 1 in above the lentils. Bring to a boil. Cover and simmer for about 20 minutes. Then turn off the heat and stir in the spinach. It will wilt down and cook in the heat of the pan.

Stir in the cashews, lemon juice, and salt. Finally, stir in the fresh cilantro.

Serve with cooked wholegrain rice or a wholegrain chapati.

NUTRITION per serving:
• 413 cals • 20 g protein • 13 g fat (2 g saturates)
• 50 g carbs (11 g total sugars) • 9 g fiber

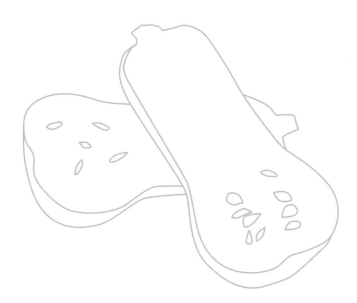

SWEET POTATO AND CHICKPEA CURRY WITH CASHEWS

This is one of my all-time favorite speedy meals. It's delicious, highly nutritious, simple, and satisfying. It provides plenty of protein and fiber, along with beta-carotene from the sweet potato and vitamin C, folate, and cancer-protective phytonutrients from the broccoli. I like to add cashews for a texture contrast, as well as to boost the iron and unsaturated fat content of the dish.

1 tbsp light olive oil or rapeseed oil

1 small onion, chopped

1–2 garlic cloves, crushed

1 tbsp medium curry paste

2 carrots, sliced

1 small sweet potato, peeled and cut into approx. $^1/_2$-in chunks

1 $^1/_2$ cups broccoli florets

1 (14 oz) can chickpeas, drained and rinsed

$^1/_3$ cup cashews

Optional: Cooked wholegrain rice, for serving

Serves 2

Heat the oil in a large heavy-bottomed pan and stir-fry the onion for 4 mins or until translucent.

Add the garlic and continue cooking for a further 30–60 seconds. Stir in the curry paste, carrots, and sweet potato and cook for 1 minute. Add approximately ¾ cup hot water, cover, and simmer for 5 minutes.

Add the remaining vegetables and chickpeas and continue cooking for 10 minutes until the vegetables are just tender, stirring occasionally, adding a little more water if necessary.

Stir in the cashews and serve with cooked wholegrain basmati rice.

NUTRITION per serving:
• 557 cals • 20 g protein • 24 g fat (4 g saturates)
• 57 g carbs (18 g total sugars) • 17 g fiber

OVEN-BAKED FALAFEL
WITH TOMATO SALSA

Falafel are perfect for al fresco eating—picnics, barbecues—as well as lunch on the move. Chickpeas are packed with protein, fiber, iron, manganese, and magnesium. They also contain fructo-oligosaccharides, which increase the friendly bacteria of the gut that improve digestion. These falafel are baked instead of fried, so they don't absorb extra oil.

1 (14 oz) can chickpeas, drained and rinsed

½ onion, very finely chopped

1 tbsp fresh cilantro, chopped

1 tbsp fresh mint or parsley, chopped

2 garlic cloves, crushed

1 tsp ground coriander

1 tsp ground cumin

1 tbsp gram flour (chickpea or lentil flour) mixed with 2 tbsp water

1 tbsp olive oil

For the salsa:

2 large ripe tomatoes, skinned

¼ red onion, finely chopped

1 tbsp fresh cilantro, finely chopped

Salt and freshly ground black pepper

Optional: Salad and wholegrain pita breads, for serving

Serves 2 (makes 12 falafels approx.)

Preheat the oven to 400 °F. Lightly oil a baking sheet.

Put the chickpeas in a blender or food processor and process for a few seconds. Add the onion, cilantro, mint or parsley, garlic, spices, gram flour paste, and olive oil. Process for a few seconds until combined and a fairly smooth, stiff purée.

Form the mixture into balls about the size of a walnut. You should be able to make about 12. Coat lightly with a little gram flour. Place on the oiled baking sheet and cook in the preheated oven for about 20 minutes until golden, turning once.

Meanwhile, make the salsa. Finely chop the tomatoes and mix with the onion and cilantro. Season to taste. Chill.

Serve the cooked falafel with the salsa, salad, and wholegrain pita breads.

NUTRITION per serving:
• 323 cals • 5 g protein • 11 g fat (1 g saturates)
• 36 g carbs (7 g total sugars) • 10 g fiber

LENTIL AND TOMATO RAGU

This is my go-to meal at the end of the week when I've run low on fresh ingredients and am searching the store cupboard for inspiration. All it requires is a packet of red lentils and a can of tomatoes and, provided you've got an onion, a carrot, and few herbs handy, you've got a nutritious and satisfying meal. Add any other vegetables you happen to have on hand—butternut squash, mushrooms, and celery work well—and serve with pasta.

1 tbsp light olive oil
1 small onion, chopped
1 large carrots, chopped
2 sticks of celery, chopped
1–2 garlic cloves, crushed
$^1/_2$ cup + 2 tbsp red lentils
$^1/_2$ (14 oz) can chopped tomatoes
1 tbsp tomato purée
$^1/_2$ tsp each: dried oregano, thyme
1 bay leaf
1 cup vegetable stock
Salt and freshly ground black pepper
$^1/_2$ cup Cheddar cheese, grated

Serves 2

Heat the oil in a nonstick heavy-bottomed pan, then add the onion, carrots, celery, and garlic and cook over a moderate heat for 5 minutes.

Add the lentils, chopped tomatoes, tomato purée, herbs, and stock. Stir and bring to a boil. Simmer for 20–30 mins until the lentils and vegetables are tender. You may need to add some water midway through cooking if the lentils absorb too much of the liquid. Season with salt and freshly ground black pepper. Scatter with the grated cheese.

NUTRITION per serving:
• 432 cals • 24 g protein • 15 g fat (6 g saturates)
• 45 g carbs (11 g total sugars) • 9 g fiber

PUY LENTIL LASAGNA

This is a long-standing family favorite in my house. I'll often make a larger quantity and keep the leftovers in the fridge or freezer for a handy "ready meal" when I have no time or am too tired to cook. It supplies lots of protein along with iron, vitamin C, and B vitamins. I have used peppers and zucchini in this recipe but you can add mushrooms, eggplant, or frozen spinach if you like. I'll often substitute a can of red kidney beans or chickpeas for the lentils for an equally nutritious supper.

1 onion, sliced

2 garlic cloves, crushed

1 red pepper, sliced

1 zucchini, thinly sliced

1 ½ cups ready-cooked Puy lentils

1 (14 oz) can chopped tomatoes

2 tbsp tomato purée

2 tsp dried mixed herbs or Herbes de Provence

1 tsp vegetable bouillon powder

¾ cup water

6–8 lasagna sheets (dry or pre-cooked)

1 tbsp grated Parmesan

For the cheese sauce:

2 ½ cups any milk of your choice

1 tbsp cornflour

1 cup grated hard cheese, such as Cheddar

Optional: Leafy salad, for serving

Serves 4

Preheat the oven to 350 °F.

Heat the oil in a large nonstick pan and fry the onion for 5 min. Add the garlic and pepper and continue cooking for a further 3–4 min. Add the zucchini and cook for a minute or two. Add the lentils, tomatoes, tomato purée, herbs, bouillon, and water, then stir and leave to simmer for 15 min If using dry lasagna noodles, cook according to package instructions.

Make the cheese sauce. In a measuring jug, mix the cornflour with a little of the milk until smooth. Pour into a saucepan and add the remaining milk. Heat gently, stirring constantly with a wooden spoon or whisk. Bring to a boil and simmer gently for one minute. Add the cheese and stir until melted.

To assemble the lasagna, put one half of the lentil mixture in the bottom of a baking dish, cover with one third of the cheese sauce, and then half the lasagna sheets. Repeat twice, finishing with a layer of cheese sauce. Top with the parmesan. Bake in the oven for 20–30 minutes or until bubbling and golden brown. Remove from the oven and allow to cool a little before serving.

Serve with a leafy salad.

NUTRITION per serving:
- 510 cals • 29 g protein • 17 g fat (9 g saturates)
- 59 g carbs (17 g total sugars) • 9 g fiber

CHICKPEA AND VEGETABLE TAGINE WITH COUSCOUS

Perfect for a mid-week refueling supper, this mildly spiced Moroccan-inspired tagine is packed with protein, vitamins, and fiber. The dried apricots soften as the dish cooks and impart the most wonderful flavor and texture contrast—not to mention lots of beta-carotene and iron. I recommend making it in advance—the flavors blend and improve. You can make a larger quantity and keep the remainder in the fridge for up to three days or in the freezer for up to three months.

1 tbsp light olive or rapeseed oil

1 onion, sliced

1 garlic clove, crushed

1 tsp ground coriander

$\frac{1}{2}$ tsp ground cumin

$\frac{1}{2}$ tsp paprika

$\frac{1}{2}$ tsp ground cinnamon

$\frac{1}{2}$–1 small chili (optional)

1 red pepper, diced

$\frac{1}{2}$ butternut squash, peeled and chopped

$\frac{1}{2}$ small eggplant, diced

1 zucchini, sliced

$\frac{1}{2}$ (14 oz) can chopped tomatoes

$\frac{1}{2}$ (14 oz) can chickpeas, drained and rinsed

$\frac{2}{3}$ cup vegetable stock

$\frac{1}{3}$ cup ready-to-eat dried apricots

A small handful of fresh cilantro, chopped

1 tbsp lemon juice

$\frac{3}{4}$ cup couscous

$\frac{1}{2}$ cup vegetable stock

$\frac{1}{2}$ cup water

Salt and freshly ground black pepper

Small handful of cilantro leaves, roughly chopped

Serves 2

Heat the olive oil in a large nonstick pan. Add the onions and cook gently for 4–5 minutes, stirring occasionally. Add the garlic, spices, and chili and stir for a few moments. Add the vegetables and continue cooking for a few minutes, then add the chopped tomatoes, chickpeas, vegetable stock, and apricots. Stir and bring to a boil. Cover then simmer for 15 minutes or until the vegetables are tender. Stir in the fresh cilantro.

While the tagine is cooking, put the couscous, stock, and water in a saucepan and bring to a boil. Remove from the heat and leave to stand for 5 minutes or until the liquid has absorbed. Fluff with a fork, then serve with the tagine.

NUTRITION per serving:
• 573 cals • 20 g protein • 11 g fat (1 g saturates)
• 87 g carbs (31 g total sugars) • 20 g fiber

LENTIL, QUINOA, AND BEAN BAKE

This highly nutritious mix of beans, lentils, and quinoa provides all the essential amino acids you need for rapid recovery after a hard training session. It's not only packed with protein but is also a good source of fiber and iron.

1 tbsp light olive oil
1 onion, chopped
½ red pepper, chopped
1 garlic clove, chopped
A handful of cherry tomatoes
⅔ cup quinoa
1 ¼ cups vegetable stock or water
½ (14 oz) can mixed beans, drained
½ (14 oz) can green or brown lentils, drained
½ (14 oz) can chopped tomatoes
A small handful of fresh cilantro, chopped

Serves 2

Heat the olive oil in a large nonstick pan and cook the onion and pepper for 3–4 minutes. Add the garlic and tomatoes and continue cooking for 2 minutes more.

Add the quinoa, stock, beans, lentils, and tomatoes. Stir and bring to a boil. Reduce the heat and simmer for about 20 minutes until the liquid has absorbed and the quinoa is cooked. Stir in the fresh cilantro.

Serve with a steamed leafy green vegetable, such as kale or spinach.

> **NUTRITION per serving:**
> • 525 cals • 28 g protein • 12 g fat (2 g saturates)
> • 70 g carbs (13 g total sugars) • 11 g fiber

MIXED BEAN AND LENTIL HOTPOT WITH FRESH CILANTRO

Beans and lentils really are one of my staple cupboard ingredients and I always make sure I have some stocked up in case I want to throw a quick supper together. They really are amazing powerhouses of nutrients, supplying fiber and protein, B vitamins, iron, manganese, and zinc. This recipe combines both of these nutritious ingredients with a few colorful vegetables for extra vitamins.

1 tbsp olive or rapeseed oil
1 onion, chopped
1 small red pepper, diced
1 garlic clove, crushed
½ cup + 2 tbsp red lentils

2 cups vegetable stock
2 carrots, sliced
½ (14 oz) can mixed beans in water, drained and rinsed
1 tbsp lemon juice

Salt and freshly ground black pepper
A small handful of fresh cilantro, finely chopped
Optional: quinoa or wholegrain rice, plain yogurt, for serving

Serves 2

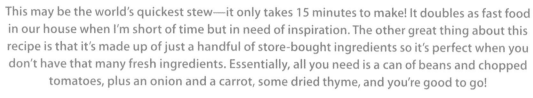

BEAN AND TOMATO STEW

This may be the world's quickest stew—it only takes 15 minutes to make! It doubles as fast food in our house when I'm short of time but in need of inspiration. The other great thing about this recipe is that it's made up of just a handful of store-bought ingredients so it's perfect when you don't have that many fresh ingredients. Essentially, all you need is a can of beans and chopped tomatoes, plus an onion and a carrot, some dried thyme, and you're good to go!

1 tbsp light olive or rapeseed oil
1 onion, sliced
1 garlic clove, crushed
1 carrot, diced
½ red pepper, diced (optional)
1 (14 oz) can chopped tomatoes
1 (14 oz) can borlotti, red kidney, or cannellini beans, drained
1 tsp vegetable bouillon
1 tsp dried thyme
2 tbsp low-fat plain Greek yogurt

Serves 2

Heat the olive oil in a large nonstick pan. Add the onion, garlic, carrots, and peppers and sauté for about 5 minutes until the vegetables have softened.

Add the tomatoes, beans, bouillon, and thyme, stir and bring to a boil. Simmer for 10 minutes until the vegetables are tender, the flavors have infused nicely, and the sauce has reduced a little.

Serve topped with a spoonful of low-fat plain Greek yogurt, basmati or wholegrain rice, and an extra green veg, such as cabbage or broccoli.

NUTRITION per serving:
• 292 cals • 18 g protein • 7 g fat (1 g saturates)
• 32 g carbs (16 g total sugars) • 13 g fiber

Heat the oil in a heavy-bottomed pan and sauté the onions for 5 minutes.

Add the red pepper and garlic and continue cooking for one minute while stirring continuously.

Add the lentils, stock, carrots, and beans. Bring to a boil. Cover and simmer for about 25 minutes, then season with salt, pepper, and lemon juice. Finally, stir in the fresh cilantro.

Serve with cooked quinoa or wholegrain rice and a spoonful of plain yogurt (if desired).

NUTRITION per serving:
• 422 cals • 23 g protein • 9 g fat (1 g saturates)
• 58 g carbs (15 g total sugars) • 13 g fiber

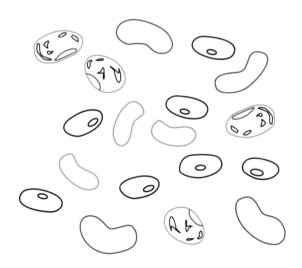

BEAN AND SPINACH BURGERS

Packed with protein, fiber, vitamins, and iron, these burgers are infinitely more nutritious and delicious than shop-bought veggie burgers. This recipe is made from store-bought standbys—canned beans and sweet corn—and frozen spinach. It makes 8 small burgers, although I often double the quantities and make a batch for the freezer.

1 tbsp light olive or rapeseed oil

1 small red onion, finely chopped

1 garlic clove, crushed

1 small red chili, deseeded and chopped (optional)

1 (14 oz) can borlotti beans, drained

1 (4 oz) can sweet corn, drained

3 ½ oz frozen chopped spinach, thawed

¾ cup fresh wholegrain breadcrumbs

½ tsp ground cumin

1 tbsp fresh cilantro, chopped

Serves 2 (makes 8 burgers approx.)

Preheat the oven to 375 °F.

Heat the oil in a nonstick frying pan. Add the onions, garlic, and chili and cook over a moderate heat for 3 minutes until softened but not browned.

Place the beans, sweet corn, spinach, breadcrumbs, cumin, and cilantro in a large mixing bowl. Add the onion mixture and mash together until well combined. Alternatively, blitz in a food processor. Shape the mixture into 8 burgers.

Place on an oiled baking tray then brush burgers with olive oil. Bake in the oven for 25–30 minutes until they are lightly browned and crisp on the outside.

Serve in wholegrain pitas or rolls and with a leafy salad.

NUTRITION per serving (4 burgers):
- 338 cals • 16 g protein • 8 g fat (1 g saturates)
- 44 g carbs (10 g total sugars), 13 g fiber

EGGPLANT, CAULIFLOWER, AND BEAN CURRY

I make this easy curry at least twice a month, although I will vary the vegetables depending on what's available and what I'm in the mood for. Cauliflower is a fantastic source of vitamin C— a quarter of a small cauliflower (the amount used in this recipe) provides 43 mg, your entire daily requirement. Eggplants contain nasunin, a potent antioxidant that protects the fatty acids needed for brain function.

1 tbsp light olive or rapeseed oil

1 onion, chopped

1 garlic clove, crushed

1 tbsp medium curry paste

½ eggplant, cut into 1-in chunks

¼ butternut squash, peeled and diced

½ small cauliflower, broken into florets

½ (14 oz) can chopped tomatoes

1 (14 oz) can red kidney beans, drained and rinsed

¾ cup + 2 tbsp water

Salt and freshly ground black pepper

A handful of fresh cilantro leaves, chopped

Serves 2

NUTRITION per serving:
• 348 cals • 17 g protein • 10 g fat (1 g saturates)
• 39 g carbs (17 g total sugars) • 19 g fiber

Heat the oil in a large pan and add the onions and cook over a moderate heat for 3 minutes until the onions have softened. Add the garlic and curry paste and cook for a minute. Add the eggplant, squash, and cauliflower and continue cooking for a further 5 minutes.

Add the tomatoes, red kidney beans, and water. Bring to a boil, then reduce the heat and simmer for 10–15 minutes until the vegetables are tender.

Season with salt and pepper. Stir in the fresh cilantro just before serving. Serve with a wholegrain chapati or roti (a flat, round Indian bread).

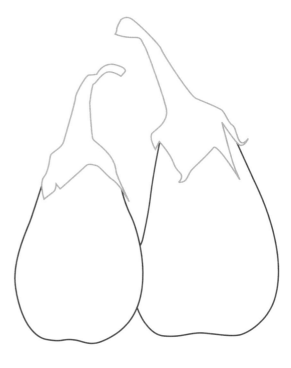

DHAL WITH ALMONDS AND FRESH CILANTRO

Dhal—essentially cooked lentils—is warming, full of flavor, and packed with nutrients. This is an incredibly easy recipe to make and only requires store cupboard spices and ingredients. Basically you just add everything to the pan and let it cook. High in fiber and protein and packed with vitamins, it's perfect for refueling after a hard workout.

1 tbsp olive oil
1 onion, chopped
1 garlic clove, crushed
$^1/_2$ tsp ground cumin
1 tsp ground coriander
$^1/_2$ cup + 2 tbsp red lentils
1 $^3/_4$ cups vegetable stock
2 carrots, diced
1 cup frozen peas
1 tbsp lemon juice
Salt, to taste
A small handful of fresh cilantro, finely chopped
$^1/_2$ cup almonds, roughly chopped and toasted
Optional: Wholegrain chapati or rice, for serving

Serves 2

Heat the oil in a heavy-bottomed pan and sauté the onions for 5 minutes. Add the garlic and spices and continue cooking for one minute.

Add the lentils, stock, and carrots. Bring to a boil. Cover and simmer for about 20 minutes, adding the peas 5 minutes before the end of the cooking time.

Stir in the lemon juice and salt. Finally, stir in the fresh cilantro and almonds. Serve with wholegrain chapatis or rice.

NUTRITION per serving:
• 537 cals • 26 g protein • 21 g fat (2 g saturates)
• 53 g carbs (14 g total sugars) • 14 g fiber

ROASTED PEPPERS WITH QUINOA AND CASHEWS

Red peppers and quinoa make perfect partners in this dish. Red peppers are fantastic sources of vitamin C (they contain more than double that of oranges), which increases the absorption of iron in the quinoa. Contrary to popular belief, quinoa isn't a grain—it is, in fact, a seed. Unlike grains, though, which lack the essential amino acids lysine and isoleucine, it contains significant amounts of all amino acids, hence its popularity with vegetarians!

2 Romano peppers

1 tbsp olive oil

1 small onion, chopped

2 garlic cloves, crushed

$2/3$ cup quinoa

1 tbsp fresh parsley, chopped

1 $1/4$ cups vegetable stock (1 tsp vegetable bouillon dissolved in hot water)

$1/3$ cup cashews, toasted

6 cherry tomatoes, halved

$1/2$ cup feta

Optional: Leafy salad, for serving

Serves 2

Heat the oven to 375 °F.

Halve the peppers and remove the seeds. Brush with a little olive oil then place them, skin-side down, in a roasting pan.

Sauté the onion and garlic in the oil for 5 minutes. Add the quinoa, parsley, and stock. Bring to a boil, then simmer for 20 minutes or until the millet grains are soft. Stir in the cashews and tomatoes. Spoon into the pepper halves and crumble the feta cheese on top. Cover the roasting pan tightly with foil and bake for 45 minutes until the peppers are tender. Serve with a leafy salad.

NUTRITION per serving:
• 523 cals • 20 g protein • 27 g fat (7 g saturates)
• 48 g carbs (15 g total sugars) • 5 g fiber

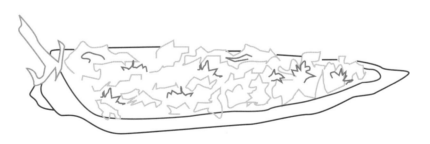

CASHEW BURGERS

These are quite wonderful burgers that you can use as a substitute for beef burgers, as filling for buns or pita breads, or simply served with a salad and rice or baked potatoes. Delicately sweet yet crunchy, cashews are packed with heart-healthy monounsaturated fats, protein, fiber, iron, magnesium, and numerous health promoting phytochemicals.

1 1/2 cups cashews

1 onion, chopped

1 carrot, chopped

2 garlic cloves, crushed

1 tbsp light olive or rapeseed oil

175 g (6 oz) fresh wholegrain breadcrumbs

3 tbsp chopped fresh cilantro or flat leaf parsley

2 eggs

1 tbsp all-purpose flour

Salt and freshly ground black pepper to taste

1/4 tsp ground cumin

Optional: Salad, brown rice, and/or baked potatoes, for serving

Makes 8

Preheat the oven to 375 °F.

Put the nuts in a food processor and pulse until roughly chopped.

Fry the onion, carrot, and garlic in the oil in a nonstick frying pan for 5–6 minutes until softened.

Place the nuts, vegetables, and remaining ingredients in a large bowl and mix together until well combined. Check the seasoning.

With your hands, divide the mixture into eight and shape into patties, approx. 3-in diameter and ½-in thick. Place them on a baking tray lined with nonstick parchment paper. Bake in the oven for 20–25 minutes until they are crisp and brown. Serve with a salad and brown rice or baked potatoes.

NUTRITION per burger:
• 197 cals • 7 g protein • 15 g fat (3 g saturates)
• 8 g carbs (3 g total sugars) • 2 g fiber

CHICKPEAS WITH SPINACH AND POTATO

Protein-powered chickpeas and iron-rich spinach are one of my favorite ingredient combinations—I'd probably put these in all my meals given half a chance! Here, I've teamed them with potatoes for an extra carb boost, useful if you'll be working out later in the day or even the next.

1 tbsp light olive or rapeseed oil

1 onion, chopped

1 garlic clove, crushed

1 red pepper, deseeded and chopped

2 medium potatoes, peeled and cut into ¾-inch chunks

1 (14 oz) can chopped tomatoes

1 cup vegetable stock

1 (14 oz) can chickpeas, drained and rinsed

2 cups fresh spinach, washed and trimmed

Optional: ½ cup Cheddar, grated, for serving

Serves 2

Heat the oil in a nonstick pan, add the onion, garlic, and red pepper, and cook over a moderate heat for 5 minutes.

Add the potatoes, chopped tomatoes, vegetable stock, and chickpeas, stir, then bring to a boil. Lower the heat and simmer for 20 minutes, stirring occasionally.

Stir in the spinach, cover, and continue cooking for a few minutes until the spinach is wilted. Add grated cheese, if desired, to serve.

NUTRITION per serving (with cheese):
- 557 cals • 24 g protein • 19 g fat (7g saturates)
- 63 g carbs (15 g total sugars) • 17 g fiber

LENTIL-STUFFED PEPPERS

There's no tastier way to obtain all your daily vitamin C quota than this super-easy dish. I like to use Romano peppers because their thinner flesh means they cook quicker than ordinary peppers, but both work equally well. Here, they are filled with cooked lentils and goat cheese, which means they're packed with fiber, protein, and iron too. You can substitute feta for the goat cheese.

2 tbsp olive oil

1 small onion, chopped

1–2 garlic cloves, crushed

1 $\frac{1}{2}$ cups pack ready-cooked Puy or beluga Lentils

4–5 baby plum tomatoes, halved

$\frac{1}{2}$ cup goat cheese, crumbled

2 Romano or red peppers

A few fresh basil leaves, roughly torn

Optional: Leafy salad and wholegrain couscous, for serving

Serves 2

Heat the oven to 375 °F.

Heat 1 tablespoon of the oil in a heavy-bottomed pan and sauté the onions for 5 minutes. Add the garlic and continue cooking for another minute. Stir in the lentils, tomatoes, and goat cheese and remove from the heat.

Cut the peppers in half lengthways, keeping the stalk attached, and remove the seeds. Brush the outsides with the remaining olive oil then place them, skin-side down, in a roasting tin. Spoon the lentil mixture into the 4 pepper halves. Cover loosely with foil.

Bake in the oven for 20–25 minutes, or until the peppers are just tender. Scatter over the basil leaves. Serve with a leafy salad and cooked wholegrain couscous.

NUTRITION per serving:
• 447 cals • 21 g protein • 20 g fat (7 g saturates)
• 40 g carbs (14 g total sugars) • 12 g fiber

RED LENTIL SHEPHERD'S PIE

Shepherd's pie strikes the perfect balance of healthy and comforting. I've used sweet potatoes for the topping as they're richer in beta-carotene than ordinary potatoes and therefore more nutritious. The vegetables and lentil filling provides lots of protein, vitamins, and minerals. I've used carrots, butternut squash, pepper, and zucchini but you can experiment with different veg.

1 tbsp olive oil

1 onion, chopped

2 garlic cloves, crushed

2 large carrots, chopped

1/2 butternut squash, peeled and chopped

1 red pepper, chopped

2 zucchini, chopped

2 tbsp fresh thyme, chopped (or 2 tsp dried)

1 1/4 cups red lentils

3 cups vegetable stock (3 tsp vegetable bouillon or 3 stock cubes dissolved in hot water)

1 (14 oz) can chopped tomatoes

3 tbsp tomato purée

Approx. 2 lb sweet potatoes, peeled and cut into chunks

2 tbsp olive oil

Salt and freshly ground black pepper

Optional: Broccoli and green beans, for serving

Serves 4

Preheat the oven to 375 °F.

Heat the olive oil in a large pan and fry the onion and garlic for 3–4 minutes until softened. Add the carrots, butternut squash, pepper, and zucchini and cook for 10 minutes. If they start sticking, add a splash of water.

Add the lentils, stock, chopped tomatoes, and tomato purée and stir. Cover and leave to simmer gently for about 20–25 minutes until the lentils are pulpy, stirring occasionally. Add a little more stock if you think it needs it.

Meanwhile, boil the sweet potatoes for 15–20 minutes until tender. Drain, then mash with the olive oil, salt, and pepper.

Spoon the lentil mixture into an ovenproof dish, top with the mash, then bake in the oven until the mashed potato starts to crisp and brown at the edges, about 20 minutes. Serve with broccoli and green beans.

NUTRITION per serving:
- 642 cals • 23 g protein • 11 g fat (2 g saturates)
- 104 g carbs (30 g total sugars) • 19 g fiber

QUINOA LENTIL BOLOGNESE

This fabulously tasty veggie version of spag bol is made even more nutritious by replacing the spaghetti with quinoa. Quinoa contains all nine essential amino acids, thus boosting the overall protein content of the meal. Brown lentils are a fantastic source of fiber, protein, iron, and magnesium.

1 tbsp light olive or rapeseed oil

1 onion, chopped

1–2 garlic cloves, crushed

1 large carrot, diced

1 zucchini, diced

$1/2$ cup + 2 tbsp dried brown or Puy lentils

1 $2/3$ cups vegetable stock (or 2 tsp vegetable bouillon dissolved in hot water)

$1/2$ (14 oz) can chopped tomatoes

1 tbsp tomato purée

1 tsp dried mixed herbs

$2/3$ cup quinoa

Optional: Cheese, grated, for serving

Serves 2

Heat the olive oil in a large pan and fry the onion for 3–4 minutes until softened. Add the garlic, carrots, and zucchini and cook for 2–3 minutes. Add the lentils, stock, chopped tomatoes, and tomato purée and stir. Bring to a boil, cover, and leave to simmer gently for about 30 minutes until the lentils are tender but not mushy and the sauce has thickened. Add a little more water or stock if it starts to stick to the pan.

Meanwhile, simmer the quinoa in 1 ½ cups water for 20 minutes until tender. Season with salt and freshly ground black pepper. Spoon into bowls and top with the lentil sauce and some grated cheese, if you like. Serve with steamed broccoli.

> **NUTRITION per serving:**
> • 542 cals • 28 g protein • 11 g fat (1 g saturates)
> • 77 g carbs (17 g total sugars) • 14 g fiber

WALNUT BURGERS

These burgers are really easy to make if you have a food processor. Walnuts are rich in omega-3 oils, which are important for oxygen delivery during exercise as well as for promoting recovery. They also supply protein, iron, vitamin E, and zinc. Substitute the eggplant for mushrooms, if you prefer. This recipe makes eight burgers so if you don't need them all, freeze the remainder (for up to three months) for another meal.

1 tbsp light olive oil or rapeseed oil

1 small onion, finely chopped

1 celery stalk, finely chopped

1 garlic clove, crushed

$1/4$ eggplant, finely chopped

1 $1/4$ cups walnuts

2–3 slices wholegrain bread

A few sprigs of fresh rosemary (or 1 tsp dried rosemary)

1 tsp yeast extract (e.g. Marmite) dissolved in 2 tbsp boiling water (or to taste)

Salt and freshly ground black pepper

2 eggs

Makes 8

Preheat the oven to 375 °F.

Heat the oil in a heavy-bottomed pan and fry the onions for 2–3 minutes. Add the celery, garlic, and eggplant and cook for 5 minutes until soft.

Place the nuts in a food processor and whiz until they are finely ground. Add the bread and process for a few seconds until they turn into breadcrumbs. Add the cooked onion mixture, rosemary, yeast extract, salt, and freshly ground black pepper. Process the mixture until it is evenly combined. Add the eggs and process until it holds together firmly. If it is too wet, add a few more breadcrumbs.

Shape the mixture into 8 equal-sized patties ½-in thick and place on an oiled baking tray. Bake in the oven for 20–25 minutes until they are crisp and brown.

Serve with baked sweet potatoes, a green vegetable (such as broccoli, kale, or Tuscan kale) and roasted slices of butternut squash (place in a baking pan, drizzle with olive oil, and bake in the oven for 20 minutes while the walnut burgers are cooking).

NUTRITION per burger:
- 216 cals • 7 g protein • 18 g fat (2 g saturates)
- 6 g carbs (2 g total sugars) • 2 g fiber

TOFU AND CHICKPEA BURGERS

These tasty protein-packed burgers are equally good warm or eaten cold in a lunch box.
I've used almonds but you can use cashews instead or even hazelnuts if you prefer.
You can also reduce or increase the amount of spices according to your taste.
I often make a batch to freeze and reheat later when I'm busy.

2 cups cooked potato, chopped
1/2 cup ground almonds (or other nuts)
1 cup (9 oz) tofu
1 (14 oz) can chickpeas, rinsed and drained
1–2 garlic cloves, crushed
1/2 small onion, chopped
10 sun-dried tomatoes, chopped finely
3/4 cup Cheddar, grated
1 egg
1/2 tsp ground cumin
1/2 tsp ground coriander
1/4 tsp cayenne pepper
Salt and freshly ground black pepper
Optional: Baked sweet potatoes,
leafy salad, for serving
Makes 8

Place all the ingredients except the egg in a food processor or blender and process for 5–10 seconds. The mixture should be fairly chunky. Alternatively, mash together with a large fork. Add the egg and process for a few seconds until combined. Shape into 8 patties with your hands.

Place them on a baking tray lined with parchment paper.
Bake in the oven for 20–25 minutes until they are crisp and brown.
Serve with baked sweet potatoes and a leafy salad.

NUTRITION per burger:
• 192 cals • 12 g protein • 11 g fat (3 g saturates)
• 10 g carbs (1 g total sugars) • 4 g fiber

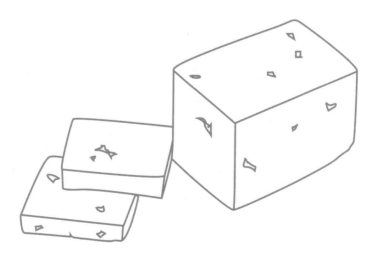

CHICKPEA AND NUT BURGERS

These tasty burgers are not only full of flavor but are also packed with protein, fiber, vitamins, and minerals—perfect athlete fuel! I recommend toasting the nuts first as this imparts a more intense flavor but, if you're short of time, just skip this step. I prefer to cook them in the oven but you can also cook them in a frying pan or on the barbecue.

$1/2$ cup hazelnuts

$1/2$ cup almonds

1 (14 oz) can chickpeas, rinsed and drained

$1/2$ tsp ground cumin

$1/4$ tsp paprika

$1/2$ tsp grated lemon rind

2 tbsp chopped fresh cilantro

1 egg, lightly beaten

1 tbsp all-purpose flour

Optional: Baked sweet potatoes, leafy salad, low-fat plain Greek yogurt, for serving

Makes 8

Preheat the oven to 375 °F.

First, toast the nuts by laying them in a single layer on a baking tray and cooking in the oven for about 10 min. Give them a stir or shake every so often and check frequently to make sure they haven't burnt.

Place the nuts in a food processor and process for about 30 seconds until roughly chopped. Add the chickpeas, cumin, and paprika and process until nearly smooth.

Transfer the mixture into a large bowl and stir in the lemon rind, cilantro, egg, and flour. Shape the mixture into 8 patties and place on an oiled baking tray. Brush burgers with a little olive oil. Bake in the oven for 25–30 minutes until they are crisp on the outside and golden.

Serve with a baked sweet potato (or in a wholegrain bun) with spinach or a leafy salad and a generous dollop of low-fat plain Greek yogurt.

NUTRITION per burger:
- 175 cals • 7 g protein • 13 g fat (1 g saturates)
- 6 g carbs (1 g total sugars) • 4 g fiber

BUTTERNUT SQUASH AND PEA RISOTTO WITH PARMESAN AND PINE NUTS

This is a perfect refueling meal after a long workout. It contains a 4 to 1 ratio of carbohydrate to protein so will restock muscle glycogen stores as well as promote rapid muscle recovery. The beans and peas supply high levels of protein and fiber, while the pine nuts give you omega-3 oils that also promote recovery.

1 tbsp light olive oil or rapeseed oil
1 small onion, chopped
1/4–1/2 red chili, finely chopped (optional)
1–2 garlic cloves, crushed
3/4 cup Arborio (risotto) rice
1/2 small butternut squash, peeled and cut into 2-cm cubes
1 3/4–2 1/2 cups hot vegetable stock (or 1 1/2 tsp vegetable bouillon dissolved in boiling water)
1/2 (14 oz) can red kidney beans
1 cup frozen peas
1/4 cup freshly grated Parmesan
1/4 cup pine nuts
Freshly ground black pepper

Serves 2

Heat the olive oil in a large heavy-bottomed pan and cook the onion over moderate heat, stirring frequently, for about 3 minutes. Add the chili and garlic and continue cooking for about 1 minute.

Add the rice and continue cooking for 1–2 minutes, stirring constantly until the grains are coated with oil and translucent.

Add the butternut squash and half of the hot vegetable stock, then bring to a boil. Reduce the heat and simmer gently until the liquid is absorbed (about 5 minutes). Add the remaining stock, a ladleful at a time, stirring and continuing to simmer until the rice is almost tender (about 15 minutes). Add the red kidney beans and peas and continue cooking for a further 5 minutes. As a guide, the total cooking time should be around 25 minutes.

Remove the pan from the heat. Stir in the grated Parmesan and pine nuts, and season with lots of freshly ground black pepper.

Serve with Parmesan shavings and extra black pepper.

NUTRITION per serving:
• 613 cals • 21 g protein • 20 g fat (4 g saturates)
• 81 g carbs (11 g total sugars) • 14 g fiber

SPINACH, BROCCOLI, AND WALNUT PASTA BAKE

This super-healthy version of macaroni cheese with added fresh veg and walnuts makes a speedy mid-week supper. Broccoli and spinach boost the iron, vitamin C, and folate content of the dish, while the walnuts supply omega-3s to promote rapid muscle recovery after exercise.

4 oz pasta

1 cup plus 4 tbsp any milk of your choice

1 heaped tbsp cornflour

$1/2$ cup mature Cheddar, grated

Salt and freshly ground pepper

4 cups spinach

1 $1/2$ cups broccoli florets

$1/2$ cup walnut pieces

Extra grated Cheddar for topping

Optional: Leafy salad, for serving

Serves 2

Cook the pasta according to the packet instructions.

Heat the 1 cup milk in a nonstick pan until hot but not quite boiling. Meanwhile, mix the cornflour with 4 tbsp milk to form a paste, then add to the pan. Stir continuously until it starts to thicken. Remove from the heat and stir in the cheese, salt, and pepper.

In a separate pan, cook the broccoli for 4–5 minutes until just tender, drain, then add the spinach. Leave for 1–2 minutes—the heat from the broccoli will wilt the spinach.

Drain the pasta, then stir in the cheese sauce, broccoli, spinach, and walnuts. Spoon into an ovenproof dish and top with a little extra cheese. Place under a hot grill for 5 mins or until the cheese melts and starts to turn golden. Serve with a leafy salad.

NUTRITION per serving:
- 654 cals • 28 g protein • 30 g fat (9 g saturates)
- 63 g carbs (10 g total sugars) • 8 g fiber

SWEET POTATO SPANISH TORTILLA

Spanish tortilla is basically a combination of eggs, potato, and vegetables. The traditional recipe uses lashings of olive oil but my version uses less oil so it's lower in calories, and sweet potato instead of ordinary potato as it contains significant levels of beta-carotene and twice as much vitamin C. This dish makes a great recovery meal as it provides a perfect ratio of carbohydrates and protein to promote speediest muscle recovery.

One medium-sized sweet potato, peeled and sliced

4 eggs

Salt and freshly ground black pepper

1 tsp chopped fresh thyme

A pinch of paprika

3 ½ cups baby spinach leaves

1 tbsp olive oil

1 small onion, thinly sliced

½ red pepper, deseeded and sliced

1 garlic clove, crushed

A small handful of fresh parsley, chopped

Optional: Leafy salad, for serving

Serves 2

Peel the sweet potato and cut into ¼-in slices. Cook in a steamer or small pan of boiling water for 5–6 minutes until just tender. Drain and set aside.

In a bowl, lightly whisk the eggs and stir in the seasoning, thyme, paprika, and spinach.

Preheat the grill to medium.

Heat the oil in an ovenproof frying pan and fry the onion, pepper and garlic over medium heat for 5 minutes or until softened. Add the sweet potato and cook for a further minute.

Pour in the egg and spinach mixture and cook over a gentle heat for 4–5 minutes until the egg starts to set. Transfer to a hot grill and cook for 2–3 minutes or until the top of the tortilla is golden and the tortilla is cooked through.

Slide the tortilla onto a plate, scatter the parsley on top, and cut into wedges. Serve with a leafy salad.

NUTRITION per serving:
- 341 cals • 16 g protein, • 17 g fat (4 g saturates)
- 27 g carbs (11 g total sugars) • 6 g fiber

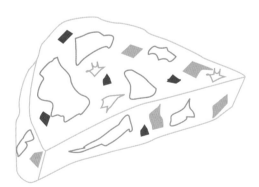

POTATO, SPINACH, AND GOAT CHEESE FRITTATA

This recipe is packed with protein—essential for repairing muscle tissue after intense exercise—as well as plenty of iron and vitamin C from the spinach. The potato adds carbohydrate to restock glycogen stores in the muscles. You can substitute another cheese, such as cheddar or cottage cheese, for the goat cheese.

1 medium potato, peeled and thickly sliced

4 large eggs

Salt and freshly ground black pepper

A little freshly grated nutmeg

4 cups fresh baby leaf spinach

1/2 cup soft goat cheese, chopped

2 tsp light olive oil

1 onion, chopped

1 garlic clove, crushed

Optional: Leafy salad, for serving

Serves 2

Cook the potato slices in a steamer or a small pan of boiling water for 5 minutes until just tender.

Beat the eggs in a large bowl and season with salt, freshly ground pepper, and nutmeg. Stir in the potatoes, spinach, and goat cheese.

Heat the olive oil in a nonstick ovenproof frying pan, then add the onions and sauté for 4–5 minutes until they are softened. Add the garlic and continue cooking for 1 minute. Pour in the frittata mixture and cook over medium heat for a few minutes until the eggs are almost set. Place the pan underneath a hot grill until the top is golden and just set.

Slide a knife around the edge and slide the frittata onto a large plate. Serve in wedges with a leafy salad.

> NUTRITION per serving:
> • 363 cals • 22 g protein • 21 g fat (8 g saturates)
> • 19 g carbs (4 g total sugars) • 4 g fiber

PASTA WITH RATATOUILLE

If you're a bit stuck in a rut of eating pasta with tomato sauce virtually every night, try this easy-to-make variation on the theme. By adding some extra peppers, eggplant, and zucchini, you can upgrade your weekday standby into something altogether more nutritious and delicious. It contains more vegetables than pasta, so it's packed with phytonutrients, fiber, and vitamin C.

1 tbsp olive oil

1 small onion, chopped

½ each: red and yellow pepper, sliced

1 garlic clove, crushed

½ eggplant, cut into ⅓-inch dice

1 small zucchini, sliced

½ (14 oz) can chopped tomatoes

Salt and freshly ground black pepper

A small handful of fresh herbs, such as parsley, oregano, thyme, and basil (or use ½ tsp of dried), chopped

4 oz wholegrain pasta

Optional: ½ cup grated cheese, for serving

Serves 2

Heat the oil in a large nonstick pan. Add the onion and peppers and cook gently for 5 minutes. Add the garlic, eggplants, zucchini, and chopped tomatoes. Stir then cover and cook over a low heat for 20-25 minutes until all the vegetables are tender, adding extra water if necessary. Season to taste with salt and freshly ground black pepper and stir in the chopped parsley.

Meanwhile, cook the pasta in boiling water according to the packet instructions. Drain.

Combine with the ratatouille and scatter the grated cheese on top, if using.

> **NUTRITION per serving:**
> • 470 cals • 19g protein • 17 g fat (7g saturates)
> • 53 g carbs (15 g total sugars) • 14 g fiber

TOFU NOODLES

This super easy noodle dish is packed with phytonutrients, including glucosinolates (in the cabbage), which have anti-cancer properties, and lots of vitamin C. The tofu adds protein and calcium. As it's all cooked over a high heat in a wok, it takes less than 15 minutes from start to finish. Perfect when you've just returned from a workout and need to eat fast!

Juice of 1 lime (or lemon)

2 tbsp water

2 tbsp soy sauce

2 garlic cloves, crushed

8 oz firm tofu, cubed

6 oz soba or rice noodles
(or use straight-to-wok noodles)

1 tbsp light olive or sesame oil

1-in piece fresh ginger, chopped

4 spring onions, chopped

1 1/2 cups green cabbage, thinly sliced

1/2 cup snow or sugar peas

Serves 2

Mix the lime (or lemon) juice, water, soy sauce, and half the garlic in a small shallow dish. Add the tofu, stir to coat in the marinade, and set aside for 30 minutes.

Cook the noodles in a saucepan according to the instructions on the packet. Drain.

Heat the oil in a wok and stir-fry the remaining garlic and ginger for 1 minute. Add the spring onions, cabbage, and snow peas and stir-fry for 2 minutes. Drain the tofu, reserving the marinade, and add to the vegetables along with the drained noodles or straight-to-wok noodles, if using. Pour the reserved marinade over the noodles and vegetables. Continue cooking for another minute. Serve.

NUTRITION per serving:
• 499 cals • 20 g protein • 13 g fat (1 g saturates)
• 73 g carbs (4 g total sugars) • 4 g fiber

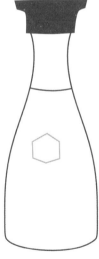

TOFU AND VEGETABLE STIR-FRY

Tofu is an excellent source of protein and calcium and can be used in place of meat in many recipes. Plain tofu is quite bland, so I recommend using a ready-made marinated tofu (available in supermarkets) in this recipe for its richer flavor.

1 tbsp light olive oil or rapeseed oil

1 onion, sliced

1 garlic clove, crushed

1 tsp fresh ginger, grated

1 red pepper, chopped

1 $^1/_2$ cups broccoli, cut into small florets

$^3/_4$ cup green cabbage, sliced

1 tbsp tamari (Japanese soy sauce)

$^1/_2$ cup water

7 oz marinated tofu, cut into $^1/_2$-in cubes

2 $^1/_2$ tbsp cashews

Optional: Wholegrain rice, for serving

Serves 2

Heat the oil in a wok until it is hot, then add the onion, garlic, and ginger and stir-fry on medium to high heat for 2 minutes.

Add the pepper, broccoli, and cabbage and stir-fry for another 2 minutes. Add the tamari and water, cook for another 2 minutes, then add the tofu. Leave to cook for 2 minutes. Remove from the heat and then stir in the cashews.

Serve with cooked wholegrain rice.

> **NUTRITION per serving:**
> • 330 cals • 20 g protein • 20 g fat (2 g saturates)
> • 14 g carbs (10 g total sugars) • 8 g fiber

What is tofu?

Tofu is made from soy milk (soy beans and water) and a coagulant, or curdling agent (usually calcium sulphate), in a process similar to cheese-making. It is high in protein—it contains all nine essential amino acids—and calcium, and is an all-star for absorbing marinades and spices. It can be used in stir-fries, salads, pasta dishes, and desserts. A 6 oz serving contains 20 g protein, the optimal amount that should be eaten after exercise and at each meal for stimulating muscle growth and recovery.

TOFU AND BLACK BEAN BURGERS

These tasty vegan burgers are packed with protein and fiber. The tofu helps to bind the ingredients together thus avoiding the need to add eggs. They are mildly spicy but if you prefer a stronger flavor, you can, of course, use extra curry paste or substitute cumin or curry powder for the paste.

7 oz firm tofu

1 tbsp korma curry paste

2 spring onions, roughly chopped

A small handful fresh parsley, roughly chopped

$1/2$ tsp paprika

Salt and freshly ground black pepper

1 (14 oz) can black beans, drained

$1/3$ cup fresh wholegrain breadcrumbs

Light olive oil or rapeseed oil for brushing

Optional: Wholegrain buns, salad leaves, avocado slices, for serving

Makes 4

Preheat the grill to medium.

Put the tofu, curry paste, spring onions, parsley, paprika, and seasoning into a food processor. Process until just combined, but not smooth. Add the beans and pulse briefly until they are roughly broken up. Tip mixture into a large bowl.

Mix in the breadcrumbs, then shape mixture into four equal patties. Place on a baking sheet, brush with oil and grill for 7–10 minutes, turning once, until golden on top and piping hot.

Serve in a wholegrain bun with salad leaves and avocado slices.

NUTRITION per serving:
- 171 cals • 12 g • 6 g fat (1 g saturates)
- 15 g carbs (1 g total sugars) • 6 g fiber

SPICED QUINOA AND TOFU PILAF

Quinoa has a low GI (glycemic index) so will curb hunger for longer and maintain blood sugar levels. It provides a good source of protein, magnesium, zinc, fiber, and vitamin E. The pepper provides plenty of vitamin C, which is good for strengthening collagen and the walls of your small blood vessels.

1 tbsp light olive oil or rapeseed oil
1 small onion, chopped
1 garlic clove, crushed
1 tsp cumin seeds
$\frac{1}{2}$ tsp turmeric
1 red pepper, chopped
$\frac{2}{3}$ cup quinoa
1 $\frac{1}{4}$ cups vegetable stock
7 oz tofu, chopped
Salt and freshly ground black pepper
2 tbsp golden raisins
A small handful of fresh cilantro leaves, roughly chopped
Optional: Leafy salad or steamed broccoli, for serving
Serves 2

Heat the oil in a large saucepan and sauté the onion over a gentle heat for 5 minutes. Add the garlic, cumin seeds, turmeric, and pepper and continue cooking for 3 minutes.

Add the quinoa and vegetable stock, stir well, bring to a boil, then reduce the heat and simmer for about 20 minutes until the liquid has been absorbed and the quinoa is tender.

Meanwhile heat a little light olive oil in a nonstick wok or pan and stir-fry the tofu for 3–4 minutes until golden on the outside. Stir into the pilaf, season with salt and black pepper. Stir in the golden raisins and cilantro.

Serve with a leafy salad or steamed broccoli.

> **NUTRITION per serving:**
> • 464 cals • 23 g protein • 16 g fat (1 g saturates)
> • 53 g carbs (21 g total sugars) • 6 g fiber

TOFU AND VEGETABLE KEBABS

These kebabs are perfect for al fresco dining and barbecues. As the vegetables are cooked only briefly and over a high heat, they retain most of their nutrients. You can also use other summer vegetables, such as pieces of corn on the cob and slices of fennel.

7 oz firm tofu
$^1/_2$ red pepper, cut into 1-in pieces
$^1/_2$ yellow pepper, cut into 1-in pieces
1 zucchini, thickly sliced
$^1/_2$ eggplant, cut into 1-in cubes
8 button mushrooms
8 cherry tomatoes

For the marinade:
2 tbsp extra virgin olive oil
2 tsp soy sauce
Grated zest and juice of 1 lime (or lemon)
$^1/_2$ tsp grated fresh root ginger
1 tsp runny honey or maple syrup
1 garlic clove, crushed
2 tbsp water
Optional: Leafy salad, baked sweet potatoes, for serving
Serves 2

Cut the tofu into 12 cubes. Place in a shallow dish along with the prepared vegetables.

To make the marinade, mix together the olive oil, soy sauce, lime (or lemon) juice, ginger, honey (or maple syrup), garlic, and water.

Spoon the marinade over the tofu and vegetables, making sure they are thoroughly coated. Leave for at least one hour, turning occasionally.

Thread the tofu and vegetables onto 8 bamboo skewers. Brush with the remaining marinade and place under a hot grill or on a barbecue for about 10 minutes, turning frequently and brushing with marinade, until slightly browned.

Serve with a leafy salad and baked sweet potatoes.

NUTRITION per serving:
• 310 cals • 18 g protein • 19 g fat (2 g saturates)
• 12 g carbs (11 g total sugars) • 8 g fiber

ROASTED ROOT VEGETABLES AND TOFU

This recipe has it all—it's inexpensive, healthy, fast, and delicious. It's one of my favourite throw-it-together-quickly meals! You basically chop up whatever root (or other seasonal) vegetables you have handy—onions, potatoes, beets, celery, and turnip also work well—cube some tofu, toss in some olive oil and whatever herbs you have on hand, and roast for 40 minutes.

2 carrots, halved

1 parsnip, quartered

1 sweet potato, peeled and sliced

¼ rutabaga, cut into wedges

¼ butternut squash, peeled and thickly sliced

1–2 garlic cloves, crushed

A few rosemary or thyme sprigs

Salt and freshly ground black pepper

2 tbsp olive oil

7 oz marinated tofu, drained and diced

2 spring onions, sliced

Serves 2

Preheat the oven to 400 °F. Prepare the vegetables and place in a large roasting pan or ovenproof dish and toss with the garlic, herbs, salt, pepper, and olive oil. Roast for 30–40 minutes until almost tender.

Spoon the tofu over the roasting vegetables and return to the oven for 10 minutes until the vegetables are tender. Scatter over the spring onions and serve.

NUTRITION per serving:
• 459 cals • 17 g protein • 20 g fat (2g saturates)
• 45 g carbs (22 g total sugars) • 16 g fiber

THE BEST NUT ROAST

Nut roasts are often regarded as a vegetarian alternative to the traditional Sunday roast, although they taste and look nothing like each other! In any case, they do make an impressive and nutritious centerpiece for a special meal. This is my basic go-to recipe, which you can adapt depending on what nuts and vegetables you have available. I've used mixed nuts in this recipe but you can substitute cashews, Brazil nuts, or almonds—they're all brilliant sources of protein, unsaturated fats, fiber, and a wealth of vitamins, minerals, and protective phytochemicals. You can also add any vegetables of your choice—celery, mushrooms, red pepper, carrots, eggplant, or zucchini.

1 onion, finely chopped

2 garlic cloves, crushed

1 tbsp olive oil

1 $^3/_4$ cups mixed nuts (e.g. hazelnuts, almonds, cashews)

1 $^3/_4$ cups wholegrain breadcrumbs

1 tsp yeast extract (e.g. Marmite) dissolved in $^1/_3$ cup hot water

$^1/_4$ lb vegetables of your choice (e.g. grated carrots or zucchini)

2 eggs

1 tsp thyme

Serves 6

Preheat the oven to 350 °F.

Sauté the onion and garlic in the oil until softened. Whizz the nuts in a food processor until thoroughly ground. In a large bowl, combine the ground nuts with the remaining ingredients.

Spoon the mixture into a lined loaf pan, cover with foil, and bake for 30 minutes. Remove the foil and bake for a further 15 minutes, until firm and golden. Cool slightly, then turn out.

Serve with roast potatoes and vegetables with gravy.

NUTRITION per serving:
• 359 cals • 16 g protein • 25 g fat (4 g saturates)
• 16 g carbs (6 g total sugars) • 3 g fiber

CHAPTER 7

DESSERTS

Clockwise from top right: *Blueberry New York-style cheesecake,
Chunky apple, date and walnut cake, Protein chocolate brownies, Banana nut bread*

BLUEBERRY NEW YORK-STYLE CHEESECAKE

This recipe is proof that you really can have your (cheese) cake and eat it! It's so delicious that it's hard to believe that it's actually good for you. It's made with quark (a virtually fat-free soft cheese) so is considerably lower in calories, fat, and sugar than traditional cheesecakes as well as a very tasty way of getting your post-workout protein. You also get a generous helping of polyphenols from the fresh blueberries, which of course promote speedy muscle recovery.

For the base:

1/2 cup graham crackers or gingersnap cookies

3 tbsp olive oil spread or butter

For the filling:

1 lb 2 oz quark (virtually fat-free soft cheese) or ricotta

2 eggs

3/4 cup low-fat plain Greek yogurt

1 tbsp cornflour

2 tbsp sugar with Stevia or 1/4 cup sugar

1 tsp vanilla extract

1 cup blueberries

Serves 8

Blitz the graham crackers or cookies in a food processor or place in a plastic bag and crush with a rolling pin to fine crumbs. Melt the olive oil spread or butter in a pan over a low heat. Remove from the heat, add the crumbs, and mix well. Press crumb mixture into an 7-in lined springform can.

Place the quark, eggs, yogurt, cornflour, sugar with Stevia (or sugar), and vanilla into mixing bowl. Blend at low speed for 1–2 minutes; scraping the sides of the bowl and mixing paddle halfway. Alternatively, beat together with a large spoon. Carefully stir in the blueberries with a large spoon.

Pour the batter into the pan; bake at 325 °F for 40–45 minutes until just set with a slight wobble. It should be cream on top with just a slight golden hint round the edges. Turn off the oven, prop open the door so that it is slightly ajar, and leave the cheesecake to cool in the oven (this prevents it cracking).

Once cool, remove from oven. Allow to cool completely before removing from the pan and keep in the fridge until you are ready to serve.

NUTRITION per serving:
- 211 cals • 14 g protein • 7 g fat (2 g saturates)
- 23 g carbs (10 g total sugars) • 1 g fiber

LEMON NEW YORK-STYLE CHEESECAKE

This cheesecake is simplicity itself—yet looks impressive enough to serve to guests.
Instead of the usual cream cheese and heavy cream, I use quark (a virtually fat-free soft cheese)
and low-fat plain Greek yogurt, which are both packed with protein. It's so delicious that
it's hard to believe this dessert is actually good for you!

For the base:

1/2 cup graham crackers
or gingersnap cookies

3 tbsp olive oil spread or butter

For the filling:

1 lb 2 oz quark (virtually fat-free soft
cheese) or ricotta

2 eggs

3/4 cup low-fat plain Greek yogurt

1 heaped tbsp cornflour

2 tbsp sugar with Stevia
or 1/4 cup sugar

1/4 cup honey

Zest and juice of 1 lemon

Blitz the graham crackers or cookies in a food processor or place in a plastic bag and crush with a rolling pin to fine crumbs. Melt the olive oil spread or butter in a pan over a low heat. Remove from the heat, add the crumbs, and mix well. Press crumb mixture into an 7-in lined springform can.

Place the quark, eggs, yogurt, cornflour, sugar with Stevia (or sugar), honey, lemon zest, and juice into mixing bowl. Blend at low speed for 1–2 minutes; scraping the sides of the bowl and mixing paddle halfway. Alternatively, beat together with a large spoon.

Pour the batter into the pan; bake at 325 °F for 40–45 minutes until just set with a slight wobble. It should be cream on top with just a slight golden hint round the edges.

Turn off the oven, prop open the door so that it is slightly ajar, and leave the cheesecake to cool in the oven (this prevents it cracking). Once cool, remove from oven. Allow to cool completely before removing from the pan and keep in the fridge until you are ready to serve.

> NUTRITION per serving:
> • 181 cals • 12 g protein • 6 g fat (2 g saturates)
> • 21 g carbs (11 g total sugars) • <1 g fiber

BLUEBERRY TOFU CHEESECAKE

This dairy-free cheesecake is made from tofu and cashews in place of the soft cheese. I've also replaced the usual biscuit base with a delicious mixture of almonds and dates. Not only is it packed with protein, calcium, and iron, but it requires no baking.

For the base:

1 cup almonds

¾ cup soft dates

½ cup blueberries

For the topping:

¾ cup cashews, soaked overnight

12 oz silken tofu

2 tbsp light olive, rapeseed, or coconut oil, melted

Zest and juice of 1 lemon

2 tbsp honey or maple syrup

Serves 8

For the base, blitz the almonds in a food processor until coarse. Add the dates and process until the mixture sticks together. Press it into the bottom of 7-in lined springform pan.

For the topping, place all the ingredients in a food processor and blitz until smooth. Pour the mixture over the biscuit base, smooth the surface, and chill in the fridge for at least 3 hours until set. Top with the blueberries.

NUTRITION per serving:
• 368 cals • 14 g protein • 22 g fat (4 g saturates)
• 27 g carbs (21 g total sugars) • 5 g fiber

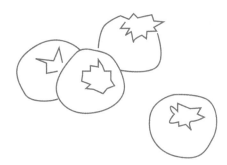

PEAR, ALMOND, AND YOGURT CAKE

This cake is made with light olive oil instead of butter. The word "light" refers to the fact that it's lighter in flavor—you won't get that olive taste, yet you still get all the healthy monounsaturated fats of olive oil. Together, the oil, ground almonds, and the Greek yogurt make the cake ultra-light and moist—as well as richer in protein than traditional cakes. The pear slices sink beautifully into the batter, creating a bit of a masterpiece, if I may say so myself!

1/4 cup + 2 tbsp light olive oil

1/4 cup sugar with Stevia or 1/2 cup sugar

2 eggs

1 1/4 cups ground almonds

1 cup self-rising flour

1 1/2 tsps baking powder

1/4 cup + 2 tbsp low-fat strained Greek yogurt

1/2 tsp almond extract

1 pear, peeled and finely sliced

Serves 8

Preheat the oven to 340 °F. Line an 8-in round cake pan with parchment paper.

In a bowl (or a mixer) mix together all the ingredients except the pear until well combined.

Spoon the mixture into the prepared pan, smooth the surface, and arrange the pear slices on top like the spokes on a wheel. Bake in the preheated oven for 30–35 minutes until well risen and golden and a skewer inserted into the center comes out clean. Leave to cool in the pan for 10 minutes, then turn out onto a wire rack to cool completely.

> NUTRITION per serving:
> • 285 cals • 8 g protein • 19 g fat (2 g saturates)
> • 19 g carbs (6 g total sugars) • 2 g fiber

WHAT IS STEVIA?

Many of the recipes in this chapter use Stevia in place of some of the sugar. Stevia, or to describe it more accurately, stevia leaf extract (steviol glycosides), is a natural sweetener which comes from the leaves of the Stevia plant grown in South America and Asia. It's a good alternative to sugar and other sweeteners as it's natural, safe, has no calories, and does not raise blood sugar levels. You can buy stevia leaf extract as a powder combined with erythritol (a sugar alcohol, or polyol, that looks similar to sugar, provides bulk yet virtually no calories) to add to drinks or in place of sugar in baking. For the dessert and snack recipes in this book, I prefer to use a blend of sugar and stevia leaf extract, such as Tate & Lyle Sugar with Stevia. As you only need to use half the quantity you would for sugar, it means that recipes will contain significantly fewer calories.

CHOCOLATE RASPBERRY BROWNIES

Here's a healthy twist on traditional chocolate brownies. I've cut the sugar and added almonds in place of some of the flour, so they're still perfectly gooey and indulgent. I've also added fresh raspberries, which provide extra vitamin C and polyphenols as well as a great contrast in texture.

$1/4$ cup + 2 tbsp olive oil spread
$2/3$ cup light brown sugar
2 eggs
½ tsp vanilla extract
$1/2$ cup ground almonds
1 cup self-rising flour
3 tbsp cocoa powder
2 tbsp milk
$1/2$ cup raspberries
2 tbsp dark chocolate chips

Makes 12

Preheat the oven to 350 °F. Line an 8 x 8-in pan with parchment paper.

In a bowl (or a mixer) mix the olive oil spread and sugar together until pale and creamy.

Add the eggs, vanilla extract, almonds, flour, cocoa, and milk and combine together. Do not over-mix, otherwise the cake may not rise well and will have a dense texture. Carefully fold in the chocolate chips and raspberries.

Spoon the mixture into the prepared pan, smooth the surface, and bake in the preheated oven for 20 minutes until risen and firm and a skewer inserted into the center comes out clean. Leave to cool in the pan for 10 minutes, then cut into 12 squares.

NUTRITION per serving:
• 170 cals • 4 g protein • 10 g fat (2 g saturates)
• 16 g carbs (10 g total sugars) • 1 g fiber

PROTEIN CHOCOLATE BROWNIES

Can a brownie actually be healthy? Yes! This recipe is richer in protein, antioxidants, and fiber and lower in sugar and fat than traditional brownies. It contains ground almonds, Greek yogurt, and chocolate whey powder, which make the brownies super-moist and surprisingly satisfying.

1/4 cup + 2 tbsp olive oil spread

1/4 cup sugar with Stevia or 1/2 cup sugar

2 eggs

1/2 tsp vanilla extract

1 cup ground almonds

1 cup self-rising flour

2 tsp baking powder

3 tbsp cocoa powder

3 tbsp chocolate whey powder

2 tbsp low-fat plain Greek yogurt

3–4 tbsp milk

1/2 cup pecans

1/3 cup raisins

Makes 12

Preheat the oven to 350 °F. Line an 8 x 8-in pan with parchment paper.

In a bowl (or a mixer) mix together the olive oil spread, sugar with Stevia (or sugar), eggs, vanilla extract, almonds, flour, baking powder, cocoa, whey powder, yogurt, and milk until well combined. You should have a soft consistency. Fold in the pecans and raisins.

Spoon the mixture into the prepared pan, smooth the surface, and bake in the preheated oven for 20 minutes until risen and firm and a skewer inserted into the center comes out clean. Leave to cool in the pan for 10 minutes, then cut into 12 squares.

NUTRITION per serving:
• 220 cals • 7 g protein • 15 g fat (2 g saturates)
• 15 g carbs (6 g total sugars) • 2 g fiber

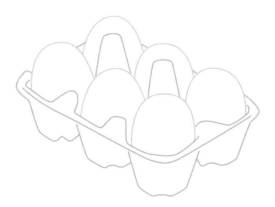

CHUNKY APPLE, DATE, AND WALNUT CAKE

Made with less sugar than a traditional cake, this recipe is naturally sweet thanks to the apples, cinnamon, and dates. I've substituted half of the usual amount of flour for oats, which boosts the fiber content, used light olive oil instead of fat to make the cake super-moist, and added a generous amount of walnuts for their excellent omega-3 value.

5 tbsp olive oil

3 tbsp sugar with Stevia
or $1/4$ cup + 2 tbsp sugar

2 tbsp brown sugar

2 eggs

1 cup all-purpose flour

1 $1/4$ cups oats

3 tsp baking powder

2 tsp ground cinnamon

3 medium eating apples,
peeled and diced

$3/4$ cup chopped walnuts

$1/3$ cup chopped dates

3–4 tbsp milk

Makes 10 slices

Preheat the oven to 325 °F. Line an 8-in round cake pan with parchment paper.

In a bowl (or a mixer) mix the olive oil, sugar with Stevia (or sugar), brown sugar, eggs, flour, oats, baking powder, and cinnamon until well combined. Mix in the apples, walnuts, dates, and enough milk so you have a fairly soft batter (this is important because the oats absorb liquid during baking).

Spoon the mixture into the prepared pan, smooth the surface, and bake in the preheated oven for 50–60 minutes until well risen and golden and a skewer inserted into the center comes out dry. Leave to cool in the pan for 10 minutes, then turn out onto a wire rack to cool completely.

NUTRITION per serving:
• 276 cals • 6 g protein • 13 g fat (2 g saturates)
• 32 g carbs (13 g total sugars) • 3 g fiber

RASPBERRY AND BLUEBERRY MUFFINS

These antioxidant-packed muffins are healthy enough to serve for dessert or as a post-workout treat. They're made with Stevia instead of sugar and I've used whey protein to replace most of the fat in the recipe. I've also replaced half of the usual flour with ground almonds to make it super-moist and supply extra protein. Best of all, they're loaded with fresh blueberries and raspberries.

3 tbsp olive oil spread
¼ cup sugar with Stevia
or ½ cup sugar
2 scoops chocolate whey protein
2 eggs
½ tsp vanilla extract
¾ cup ground almonds
¾ cup self-rising flour
1 tsp baking powder
1 tbsp cocoa powder
4–5 tbsp milk
⅓ cup blueberries
⅓ cup raspberries
3 tbsp dark chocolate chips

Makes 12

Preheat the oven to 375 °F. Line a 12-cup muffin pan with paper muffin cups.

In a bowl (or a mixer) mix the olive oil spread and sugar with Stevia (or sugar) together until pale and creamy.

Add the whey protein, eggs, vanilla extract, almonds, flour, baking powder, cocoa, and milk and combine together. Do not over-mix, otherwise the muffins may not rise well and will have a dense texture. Gently fold in the berries and chocolate chips.

Spoon the mixture into the muffin cups. Bake in the preheated oven for 18–20 minutes until risen and firm. Leave to cool in the tin for a few minutes, then cool on a wire rack.

NUTRITION per serving:
• 150 cals • 6 g protein • 8 g fat (2 g saturates)
• 12 g carbs (5 g total sugars) • 1 g fiber

CHOCOLATE AVOCADO MOUSSE

The combination of avocados and chocolate may sound a little strange but trust me, it makes the thickest, most delicious mousse. Don't worry, it doesn't actually taste of avocado at all. Best of all, it's packed with healthy monounsaturated fats, vitamin E, fiber, and polyphenols (from the cocoa powder). It contains no added sugar as the bananas and dates provide sufficient natural sweetness.

1 ripe avocado
1 ripe banana
¼ cup soft dates (e.g. Medjool)
1–2 tbsp cocoa powder

Serves 2

Slice the avocados in half and remove the stones. Using a spoon, scoop the avocado flesh from the shell and add to a food processor or blender. Add the other ingredients, then blend until completely smooth. Add a splash of water if it seems too thick. Serve in small ramekins or glass bowls.

NUTRITION per serving:
• 328 cals • 5 g protein • 17 g fat (4g saturates)
• 35 g carbs (28 g total sugars) • 8 g fiber

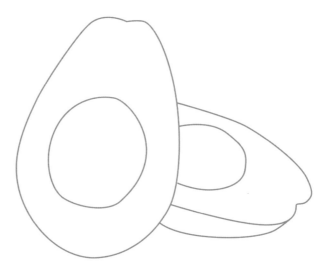

APPLE AND WALNUT CRUMBLE

This is, by far, the most popular dessert in my house. I make it practically every week throughout autumn and winter, each time with a subtle variation. The walnuts are a terrific way of adding omega-3s to your diet but you can substitute raisins, dried apricots, or dates if you prefer. The crumble can be infinitely varied too, replacing the ground almonds with chopped hazelnuts or sunflower seeds. And, of course, you can replace all or some of the apples with plums, pears, rhubarb, blueberries, or blackberries (or any combination), whatever is in season.

$1/2$ cup walnut pieces

1½ lb (about 6–7) cooking apples

2 tbsp sugar with Stevia or $1/4$ cup sugar

1 tsp ground cinnamon

2 tbsp boiling water

For the crumble:

$3/4$ cup all-purpose flour

3 tbsp sugar with Stevia or 6 tbsp light brown sugar

$1/2$ cup oats

$1/4$ cup olive oil spread or butter

$1/2$ cup ground almonds

Optional: Custard or Greek yogurt, for serving

Serves 6

Preheat oven to 375 °F.

Place the walnuts on a baking tray and toast in the oven for 5–7 minutes. Allow to cool.

Peel, core, and thinly slice the apples, and place in a large bowl. Add the walnuts, sugar with Stevia (or sugar), and cinnamon and mix. Transfer into a 4-cup ovenproof dish. Pour over the boiling water.

To prepare the crumble, place the flour, sugar with Stevia (or brown sugar), and oats in a mixing bowl. Add the spread/butter and ground almonds and rub into the mixture until it resembles breadcrumbs. Alternatively, mix together in a food processor.

Scatter the topping over the apples and bake for 40–45 minutes until golden brown. Serve with a spoonful of homemade custard or Greek yogurt.

NUTRITION per serving:
- 363 cals • 7 g protein • 19 g fat (3 g saturates)
- 39 g carbs (16 g total sugars) • 5 g fiber

BANANA NUT BREAD

I've always loved banana bread—it's a long-standing favorite in my house—so I was inspired to adapt it and make it healthier. In this recipe, I've substituted light olive oil and Greek yogurt for the butter, replaced the sugar with the natural sweetener Stevia, and added some dates to help sweeten the bread. I also opted to add walnuts as they're loaded with omega-3 fats.

2 ¼ cups all-purpose flour

3 tsp baking powder

1 tsp ground cinnamon

4 tbsp light olive oil

2 tbsp low-fat plain Greek yogurt

¼ cup sugar with Stevia
or ½ cup light muscovado sugar

1 tsp vanilla extract

2 eggs

2 ripe bananas

½ cup soft dates

1 cup walnut pieces

Makes 10 slices

Preheat the oven to 325 °F. Line a 2-lb loaf pan with parchment paper.

Place the flour, baking powder, cinnamon, olive oil, Greek yogurt, sugar with Stevia (or sugar), vanilla extract, and the eggs into a large mixing bowl. Mash the bananas and chop the dates (kitchen scissors are easiest for this) and add to the bowl. Beat the mixture for 2–3 minutes, using a wooden spoon or hand-held mixer, until well blended. Fold in the walnut pieces.

Spoon the mixture into the prepared pan and level the top. Bake for 1 hour or until a skewer inserted in the center comes out clean. If not set, bake for a further 10 minutes. Leave in the pan for 15 minutes, then turn out onto a wire rack to cool.

NUTRITION per serving:
- 285 cals • 6 g protein • 13 g fat (2 g saturates)
- 35 g carbs (14 g total sugars) • 3 g fiber

CHAPTER 8

SWEET SNACKS

Clockwise from top right: Almond cherry cookies, Fruit and nut bars, Raw energy balls, Super oat bars

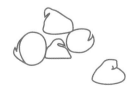

CHOCOLATE RAW ENERGY BARS

Here's a chocolate-themed variation of the Raw energy balls (page 178). They contain no added sugar, they're rich in fiber and protein, and are packed with polyphenols (from the cocoa), which are known to aid recovery and improve performance.

1 cup soft "ready-to eat" or Medjool dates

1 cup macadamia nuts (or any other variety)

⅓ cup raisins

1 cup ground almonds

1 tbsp cocoa powder

3 tbsp dark chocolate chips

2–3 tbsp water

Makes 12

Place the dates in a small saucepan with enough water to just cover. Cook the dates for about 5 minutes until soft. Drain off most of the water, then place them in a food processor with the macadamia nuts, raisins, almonds, and cocoa powder and process to a course texture.

Add the chocolate chips and water and pulse until it forms the consistency of stiff cookie dough.

Scrape out of the processor and roll between two sheets of parchment paper or plastic wrap to a ½-in thickness and cut into bars. Alternatively you can roll into balls.

Wrap each bar in plastic wrap and store in the fridge for up to a week.

> NUTRITION per serving:
> • 230 cals • 4 g protein • 15 g fat (2 g saturates)
> • 18 g carbs (15 g total sugars) • 3 g fiber

DATE AND CASHEW BARS

This is my favorite adaptation of the Raw energy balls (page 178) and the one that I turn to time and time again. They're my go-to pre- and post-exercise snack, packed with protein, essential fats, vitamins, minerals, and fiber—exactly what your muscles need after a tough workout!

1 ¼ cups soft "ready-to eat" or Medjool dates

2 cups cashews

1 cup ground almonds

2 tbsp cocoa powder

2–3 tbsps water

Makes 16

NUTRITION per serving:
• 208 cals • 6 g protein •13 g fat (2 g saturates)
• 16 g carbs (11 g total sugars) • 3 g fiber

Put the dates, cashews, almonds, and cocoa powder in a food processor and process until crumbly and evenly combined.

Add the water one tablespoon at a time until it forms the consistency of stiff cookie dough.

Scrape out of the processor and roll between two sheets of parchment paper or plastic wrap to a ½-in thickness and cut into bars. Alternatively you can roll into balls or press it into an 7 x 7-in baking pan lined with plastic wrap.

Cut into 16 bars. Wrap each bar in plastic wrap and store in the fridge for up to a week.

RECOVERY BARS

These bars are made from oats, nuts, dried fruit, and peanut butter, and provide the perfect combination of protein, carbohydrate, unsaturated fats, and antioxidants that you need for rapid recovery after training. They're very moreish—so be warned!

$^1/_2$ cup maple syrup

Scant 1 cup peanut butter (or any other nut butter)

1 cup any type of nuts, lightly toasted and coarsely chopped

1 $^1/_2$ cups rolled oats

2 tbsp ground flax, pumpkin, or chia seeds

$^2/_3$ cup dried mixed fruit, such as cranberries and apricots, coarsely chopped

Makes 12

Put the maple syrup and peanut butter in a small saucepan and heat gently until melted.

In a large bowl or food mixer, mix together the nuts, oats, flaxseeds, and dried fruit. Stir in the maple syrup and peanut butter mixture and mix until well combined. Press evenly and firmly into a 7 x 7-in baking pan lined with parchment paper, and chill until set. Cut into bars.

NUTRITION per serving:
- 283 cals • 10 g protein • 17 g fat (3 g saturates)
- 20 g carbs (11 g total sugars) • 4 g fiber

NUTTY BARS

The idea for these protein-packed bars came from 9 Bars, which I rate highly compared with other snack bars as they're low in sugar and jam-packed with nuts. My version is made with nuts—you can either buy them roasted or raw then roast in the oven—held together with just a little honey and sugar. Nuts are fantastic sources of essential fatty acids, protein, fiber vitamins, and minerals.

2 $^1/_3$ cups mixed roasted nuts

3 tbsp rapeseed, light olive oil, or coconut oil

3 tbsp runny honey

2 tbsp light brown sugar

3½ oz 85% cocoa dark chocolate

Makes 12

Preheat the oven to 350 °F. Line an 8 x 8-in-square baking pan with parchment paper.

Place the nuts in a food processor, pulse briefly until they are roughly chopped.

Add the oil, honey, and brown sugar and stir.

Spoon into the prepared baking pan, press down lightly, and bake for about 15 minutes until lightly golden but not brown around the edges.

Break the chocolate into small pieces, place in a microwavable bowl and heat on full power for 1 minute until almost molten. Stir and leave for a few moments until it is completely melted. Spread over the nut mixture. Allow to cool before cutting into bars.

> **NUTRITION per serving:**
> • 271 cals • 8 g protein • 20 g fat (3 g saturates)
> • 14 g carbs (13 g total sugars) • 3 g fiber

SUPER OAT BARS

Oat bars are hard to beat when it comes to healthy pre-workout snacks. The combination of oats, nuts, and dried fruit provide sustained energy, so you'll be able to train harder and keep going longer. Add whatever dried fruit takes your fancy and you have a super-nutritious oat bar!

$1/2$ cup olive oil spread
$1/3$ cup crunchy peanut butter
6 tbsp brown sugar
$1/3$ cup honey
2 $1/2$ cups rolled oats
1 tsp cinnamon
1 cup nuts, such as chopped walnuts, pecans, and sliced almonds
1 cup dried fruit, such as raisins, chopped dates, or apricots

Makes 16

Preheat the oven to 350 °F. Line a 9-in square baking pan with parchment paper.

Put the olive oil spread, peanut butter, sugar, and honey in a nonstick saucepan and heat together, stirring from time to time, until the mixture has melted. Remove from the heat.

In a large bowl, mix the oats, cinnamon, nuts, and dried fruit. Add the melted mixture and mix until thoroughly combined.

Transfer the mixture into the prepared pan, level the surface, and bake in the oven for 20–25 minutes until golden brown around the edges but still soft in the middle. Leave in the pan to cool. Turn out and cut into 16 squares with a sharp knife.

NUTRITION per serving:
• 265 cals • 5 g protein • 16 g fat (2 g saturates)
• 24 g carbs (15 g total sugars) • 3 g fiber

FRUIT AND NUT BARS

These bars not only taste far better than shop-bought energy bars but the nuts and oats also help prevent a blood sugar spike so you get more prolonged energy. They're packed with protein, essential fats, vitamins, and minerals and make a perfect pre- or post-workout snack.

1 cup soft "ready-to eat" or Medjool dates

2 tbsp honey

½ tsp ground cinnamon

1 ¼ cups rolled oats

⅔ cup chopped roasted hazelnuts

⅔ cup sliced almonds

⅓ cup chopped walnuts

⅓ cup raisins

A pinch of salt

Makes 12

Heat the oven to 375 °F. Line a 9-in square baking pan with parchment paper.

Place the dates in a small saucepan with enough water to just cover. Cook the dates for about 5 minutes until soft. Drain off most of the water and purée with the honey in a food processor until smooth.

Mix the cinnamon, oats, nuts, raisins, and salt in a large bowl, add the date purée and mix until well combined. Press the mixture into the lined pan, smoothing the surface so it is even on all sides. Bake for 20 minutes or until the mixture feels firm and the edges are just starting to come away from the sides.

Cool in the pan then cut into bars. They can be stored for up to a week in an airtight container.

NUTRITION per serving:
• 228 cals • 5 g protein • 11 g fat (1 g saturates)
• 25 g carbs (17 g total sugars) • 4 g fiber

DATE CRUMBLE BARS

I have to confess to a serious weakness for these bars. Smooth puréed dates sandwiched between two layers of glorious oaty crumble. Dates are a brilliant source of fiber as well as magnesium, which is known for its anti-inflammatory effects and speeding recovery after intense training.

1 ¼ cups soft ready-to-eat dates
½ cup water
½ cup olive oil spread
1 ¼ cup all-purpose flour
1 ¼ cups rolled oats
6 tbsp brown sugar
3 tbsp sugar with Stevia or ¼ cup + 2 tbsp sugar

Makes 16

Heat oven to 350 °F. Line an 8-in square pan with parchment paper.

Put the dates and water in a pan and heat gently, stirring occasionally until the dates are soft and have absorbed most of the water (about 5–10 minutes). Let cool and then purée using a hand blender or food processor until mixture forms a paste (a few lumps are ok). Add more water if required. Leave mixture to cool.

For the crumble, rub the olive oil spread into flour until it resembles breadcrumbs. This can be done by hand or in a mixer or food processor. Stir in oats, brown sugar, and sugar with Stevia (or sugar) and mix well. Press about two-thirds of the mixture firmly into the pan. Spread the filling evenly over. Sprinkle the remaining crumble evenly over the top and press down gently.

Bake for 25–30 minutes until golden brown. Cool, then cut into 16 squares.

> **NUTRITION per serving:**
> • 195 cals • 2 g protein, 7 g fat (1 g saturates)
> • 30 g carbs (16 g total sugars) • 2 g fiber

WHAT IS STEVIA?

Many of the recipes in this chapter use a blend of sugar and stevia leaf extract (see page 156). As you only need to use half the quantity you would for sugar, it means that recipes will contain significantly fewer calories.

RAW ENERGY BALLS

The inspiration for these balls comes from Nakd Bars, of which I'm a big fan. The best thing about these balls is their simplicity; they contain no added sugars, just dried fruit and nuts—so incredibly healthy. I experimented with ratios and found that almost equal parts of dried fruit to nuts works best. Here's the basic recipe, which you can adapt using any of the suggestions below. I recommend using soft ready-to-eat dates or Medjool dates, which are easier to process in the food processor.

2 cups your favorite nuts

1 ¼ cups soft ready-to-eat or Medjool dates (or a mixture of dates and raisins)

2–3 tbsp water

½–1 tsp cinnamon

Makes 16

Combine all the ingredients in a food processor. Pulse a few times just to break them up. Process for 30 seconds until the ingredients have broken down into crumb-sized pieces. Scrape the edges of the bowl and the blade if necessary. You may need to add a little extra water if the dates are quite hard. Continue processing for another 1–2 minutes, until the ingredients clump together and form a ball.

Press into a thick square, roughly 7 x 7-in in size, on a piece of plastic wrap or parchment paper. Wrap and chill in the fridge for at least an hour (this is optional). Shape into small balls, then wrap each one in plastic wrap. Store in the fridge for several weeks or in the freezer for up to three months.

Try these combinations: Macadamia-cherry-almond, date-almond-cashew, date-raisin-pecan, date-walnut.

Try these extras: Shredded coconut, chia seeds, chocolate chips, cocoa powder, vanilla, crystallized ginger, ground nutmeg, or lemon zest.

> NUTRITION per serving:
> • 172 cals • 5 g protein • 11 g fat (1 g saturates)
> •13 g carbs (10 g total sugars) • 3 g fiber

ALMOND, FIG, AND CASHEW ENERGY BARS (VG)

These bars are packed with protein and slow-release carbs so are a great way to fuel your workouts. Dates and nuts make up the base of these bars, while figs and vanilla add extra calcium and fiber. If you have trouble finding ready-to-eat soft dates, soak ordinary dried dates overnight in water before adding to the food processor.

1 $\frac{1}{3}$ cups cashews
1 cup ground almonds
$\frac{3}{4}$ cup soft ready-to-eat or Medjool dates
$\frac{1}{2}$ cup ready-to-eat dried figs
$\frac{1}{2}$–1 tsp vanilla extract
2–3 tbsp water

Makes 12

Process the cashews in a food processor for about 30 seconds. Add the almonds, dates, figs, and vanilla extract and process until crumbly and evenly combined. Add the water one tablespoon at a time and continue processing until the ingredients clump together and form a ball.

Turn the mixture out of the processor and press into an 7 x 7-in baking pan lined with plastic wrap or parchment paper. It should be approximately $\frac{1}{3}$-in thick. Cut into bars, then wrap each bar in plastic wrap and store in the fridge for several weeks or in the freezer for up to three months.

The dough can also be shaped into small "energy balls."

NUTRITION per serving:
• 213 cals • 6 g protein • 13 g fat (2 g saturates)
• 17 g carbs (13 g total sugars) • 3 g fiber

ALMOND AND PUMPKIN SEED OAT BARS

These tasty oat bars are made extra healthy by the addition of almonds and pumpkin seeds, which provide essential fatty acids, minerals, and protein. Almonds are a perfect food for athletes—they're high in protein, fiber, healthy monounsaturated fats, vitamin E, calcium, magnesium, potassium, flavanoids; they satisfy the appetite, and ward off hunger pangs. I've also substituted half the usual amount of olive oil spread for almond butter for an extra protein boost.

¼ cup olive oil spread

⅓ cup almond butter

6 tbsp brown sugar

⅓ cup honey

2 ½ cups rolled oats

1 ½ cups sliced almonds

⅓ cup pumpkin seeds

⅓ cup soft ready-to-eat or Medjool dates, chopped

Makes 16

Preheat the oven to 350 °F. Line a 9-in-square baking pan with parchment paper.

Put the olive oil spread, almond butter, brown sugar, and honey in a nonstick saucepan and place over a low heat, stirring from time to time, until the ingredients have melted. Remove from the heat.

In a large bowl, mix the oats, almonds, pumpkin seeds, and dates. Add the melted mixture and mix together. Transfer the mixture into the prepared pan, level the surface, and bake in the oven for 20–25 minutes until golden brown around the edges but still soft in the middle.

Leave in the pan to cool. Turn out and cut into 16 squares with a sharp knife.

> **NUTRITION per serving:**
> • 228 cals • 6 g protein • 12 g fat (2 g saturates)
> • 22 g carbs (12 g total sugars) • 3 g fiber

PEANUT BUTTER COOKIES

If you're a peanut butter fan, then you'll love this recipe. I've substituted oats for some of the flour in traditional cookie recipes. As a result, the cookies are considerably higher in protein, monounsaturated fats, fiber, vitamins, and minerals than conventional cookies.
What's more, they contain very little sugar if you use stevia leaf extract rather than brown sugar.

1 cup crunchy peanut butter
$^1/_4$ cup sugar with Stevia
or $^3/_4$ cup dark brown sugar
$^1/_4$ cup + 2 tbsp olive oil spread
1 tbsp maple syrup
$^1/_2$ tsp vanilla extract
1 cup rolled oats
$^3/_4$ cup all-purpose flour
$^1/_2$ egg, beaten
$^1/_3$ cup raisins

Makes 15

Preheat the oven to 375 °F and line one or two baking trays with parchment paper.

Place all the ingredients except the egg and raisins in a large mixing bowl and mix on low speed until combined. Alternatively, beat together with a wooden spoon.

Add the beaten egg and raisins, then mix together until you have a smooth, fairly stiff dough.

Roll heaped teaspoonfuls of the mixture into balls, approx. 1¼-in diameter. Place on the baking trays, about 1 in apart, then flatten lightly with your hand.

Bake for 12–14 minutes or until light golden. Cool for a few minutes before transferring to a wire rack.

NUTRITION per serving:
• 143 cals • 4 g protein • 9 g fat (2 g saturates)
• 11 g carbs (5 g total sugars) • 1 g fiber

ALMOND AND CHERRY COOKIES

This is my all-time favorite cookie recipe that I keep going back to time and time again. Made principally from almonds and oats, it uses very little sugar so it has a lower GI than conventional cookies, and considerably more fiber. Almonds are also good sources of monounsaturated fats and calcium, so pop these cookies in your bag when you need a pre-workout boost.

1 cup ground almonds
¼ cup sugar with Stevia or ½ cup sugar
¼ cup + 2 tbsp olive oil spread
1 tbsp maple syrup or golden syrup
½ tsp vanilla extract
¾ cup all-purpose flour
1 cup rolled oats
½ egg, beaten
¼ cup candied cherries, cut into quarters

Makes 15

Preheat the oven to 375 °F and line one or two baking sheets with parchment paper.

Place all the ingredients except the egg and cherries in a mixer bowl and mix on low speed until combined.

Add the beaten egg and cherries, then mix together until you have a smooth soft dough.

Shape the dough into about 15 balls, approx. 1 ¼-in diameter. Place on the baking sheets, about 1 in apart, then flatten lightly with your hand. Bake for 12–14 minutes or until light golden.

NUTRITION per serving:
• 156 cals • 3 g protein • 9 g fat (1 g saturates)
• 15 g carbs (5 g total sugars) • 1 g fiber

CHOCOLATE CHIP OAT COOKIES

Anything containing chocolate chips has to be a winner—and these cookies are no exception! Not only are they deliciously soft and chewy with glorious bites of chocolate, they're surprisingly healthy. The addition of oats means they're higher in fiber and B vitamins than shop-bought cookies, and are perfect for snacking on when you want an energy boost.

¼ cup + 2 tbsp olive oil spread

6 tbsp brown sugar

2 tbsp clear honey or golden syrup

½ tsp vanilla extract

¾ cup all-purpose flour

1 cup rolled oats

¼ cup plain chocolate chips

Makes 12

Preheat the oven to 375 °F and line a baking sheet with parchment paper.

Mix together the olive oil spread, sugar, and honey/golden syrup until smooth using either a mixer or wooden spoon.

Add the vanilla extract, flour, and oats to the mixture and continue mixing until the mixture comes together to form a stiff dough. Stir in the chocolate chips and mix until evenly combined.

Form the dough into approx. 12 small balls (about the size of a Ping Pong ball), placing them about 1 in apart on the baking sheet. Flatten gently with the palm of your hand. Bake for about 12 minutes or until light golden.

NUTRITION per serving:
- 160 cals • 2 g protein • 7 g fat (2 g saturates)
- 21 g carbs (10 g total sugars) • 1 g fiber

APRICOT AND ALMOND COOKIES

These cookies are a clever way of boosting your beta-carotene, fiber, and iron intake as they include delicious dried apricots, which are naturally rich in these nutrients. I like to use apricots that are naturally dried rather than preserved with sulphur dioxide (look for organic on the label). They have a rich, intense flavor and a lovely naturally dark color.

1/4 cup + 2 tbsp olive oil spread
1/4 cup sugar with Stevia or
1/2 cup sugar
1 cup ground almonds
1 tbsp maple syrup or golden syrup
1/2 tsp almond extract
2/3 cup all-purpose flour
1 1/4 cups rolled oats
1/2 egg, beaten
2/3 cup soft dried apricots, chopped

Makes 15

Preheat the oven to 375 °F and line one or two baking sheets with parchment paper.

Place all the ingredients except the egg and apricots in a mixing bowl and mix on low speed until combined. Add the beaten egg and apricots, then mix together until you have a smooth soft dough.

Shape the dough into about 15 balls, approx. 1¼-in diameter. Place on the baking sheets, about 1-in apart, then flatten lightly with your hand. Bake for 12–14 minutes or until light golden.

NUTRITION per serving:
• 162 cals • 4 g protein • 9 g fat (1 g saturates)
• 16 g carbs (6 g total sugars) • 2 g fiber

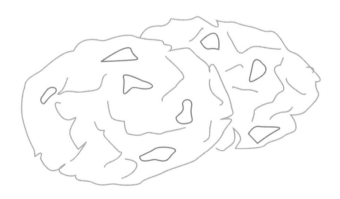

COCONUT COOKIES

The idea for these cookies came from the iconic Anzac biscuits, which were originally made to send overseas to the ANZACs (Australian and New Zealand Army Corps) serving in World War I. The combination of coconut and oats produces a lower GI than traditional biscuits so you'll get sustained energy, not a quick fix.

1/4 cup + 2 tbsp olive oil spread
3 tbsp sugar with Stevia or 6 tbsp sugar
1 tbsp clear honey or golden syrup
½ tsp vanilla extract
3/4 cup all-purpose flour
1 cup rolled oats
Heaping cup shredded coconut

Makes 15

Preheat the oven to 375 °F and line one or two baking sheets with parchment paper.

Beat together the olive oil spread and sugar until light and smooth using a mixer or with a wooden spoon.

Beat in the golden syrup and vanilla extract. Add the flour, oats, and coconut to the mixture, mixing well. Place spoonfuls on to the baking sheets, about 1 in apart, then flatten with your hand. Bake for 10–12 minutes or until light golden.

NUTRITION per serving:
• 146 cals • 2 g protein • 9 g fat (4 g saturates)
• 13 g carbs (3 g total sugars) • 2 g fiber

HAZELNUT COOKIES

Hazelnut butter is full of healthy, unsaturated fats, protein, fiber, vitamins, and minerals. Here I've substituted half the usual amount of fat for hazelnut butter—you can use more if you prefer a crumblier cookie.

2/3 cup crunchy hazelnut butter
6 tbsp sugar with Stevia or 3/4 cup sugar
3 tbsp olive oil spread
1 tbsp maple syrup or golden syrup
½ tsp vanilla extract
1 1/4 cups all-purpose flour
½ egg, beaten

Makes 15

Preheat the oven to 375 °F and line one or two baking sheets with parchment paper.

Place all the ingredients except the egg in a mixer bowl and mix on low speed until combined. Add the beaten egg and mix together until you have a smooth soft dough.

Take spoonfuls of the dough and shape into balls, approx. 1¼-in diameter, using your hands. Place on to the baking sheets, about 1 in apart, then flatten lightly with your hand. Bake for 12–14 minutes or until light golden.

NUTRITION per serving:
• 148 cals • 3 g protein • 9 g fat (1 g saturates)
• 14 g carbs (4 g total sugars) • 1 g fiber

CHAPTER 9

SAVORY SNACKS, SHAKES & SMOOTHIES

Left: *Berry blast smoothie*

GUACAMOLE

Avocados are packed with health-enhancing nutrients: monounsaturated oils, vitamin E, folic acid, and potassium. Guacamole also makes a good sandwich filling, a dip for vegetables, or a topping on salads.

1 ripe avocado

1 tbsp lemon or lime juice

1/2 small red onion, finely chopped

1 garlic clove, crushed

1 medium tomato, skinned and chopped

1 tbsp fresh cilantro, finely chopped

Sea salt and freshly ground black pepper

Cayenne pepper and olive oil, to serve

Serves 2

Halve the avocado and scoop out the flesh. Mash with the lemon or lime juice. Add the remaining ingredients, mixing well. Alternatively, you may process the ingredients in a food processor to a coarse purée. Check the seasoning, adding a little more black pepper or lemon juice if necessary. Sprinkle with a little cayenne pepper and drizzle with olive oil.

Serve with vegetable crudités.

NUTRITION per serving:
- 174 cals • 2 g protein • 15 g fat (3 g saturates)
- 6 g carbs (4 g total sugars) • 5 g fiber

BUTTER BEAN DIP

This dip is perfect with crudités, as well as a spread for toast. It's super quick to make and a fantastic source of protein, iron, and fiber. Keep any remainder covered in the fridge for up to three days.

1 (14 oz) can butter beans, drained and rinsed

1 garlic clove, crushed

Juice of 1/2 lemon

2 tbsp olive oil

1–2 tbsp water

Salt and freshly ground black pepper

1 tbsp chopped fresh mint or parsley

Serves 4

Put the butter beans in a food processor or blender with the garlic, lemon juice, and olive oil. Whiz until smooth, add salt and freshly ground black pepper, and process again. Add a little water if it's too thick.

Stir in the mint or parsley. Spoon into a shallow dish and chill in the fridge before serving.

NUTRITION per serving:
- 112 cals • 5 g protein • 6 g fat (1 g saturates)
- 8 g carbs (1 g total sugars) • 4 g fiber

HUMMUS

Hummus is super-quick to make with a food processor or blender, infinitely nicer than shop-bought, and healthier too. I like to add pine nuts and a few whole chickpeas to give it a more interesting texture.

1 (14 oz) can chickpeas, drained and rinsed, or ½ cup dried chickpeas, soaked overnight then boiled for 45 minutes

1–2 garlic cloves, crushed

2 tbsp extra virgin olive oil

1 tbsp tahini (sesame seed paste)

Juice of ½ lemon

2–4 tbsp water

Salt and freshly ground black pepper

1 tbsp pine nuts

Serves 4

Drain and rinse the chickpeas. Reserve 1–2 tablespoons of chickpeas. Put the remainder in a food processor or blender with the garlic, olive oil, tahini, lemon juice, and water. Whiz until smooth, add salt and freshly ground black pepper, and process again. Taste to check the seasoning. Add extra water if necessary to give the desired consistency.

Meanwhile lightly toast the pine nuts under a hot grill for 3–4 minutes until they are lightly colored but not brown (watch carefully as they color quickly).

Stir in the reserved whole chickpeas. Spoon into a shallow dish. Scatter over the pine nuts and drizzle over a few drops of olive oil. Chill in the fridge before serving.

It will keep in the fridge for up to three days.

NUTRITION per serving:
- 196 cals • 7 g protein • 14 g fat (2 g saturates)
- 10 g carbs (1 g total sugars) • 4 g fiber

BABA GHANOUSH

This eggplant dip has a delicate, slightly nutty flavor and is excellent with vegetable crudités. Eggplants, the base of this dip, are low in calories and rich in potassium and folic acid. Tahini is a sesame seed paste, packed with unsaturated fats, vitamin E, and calcium.

1 medium eggplant

Juice of ½ lemon

2 tbsp tahini

2 tbsp olive oil

1 garlic clove, crushed

Salt and freshly ground black pepper

Serves 4

Prick the eggplant all over with a fork then place under a moderate grill, turning frequently until the skin is slightly charred. Allow to cool.

Cut in half lengthways and scrape out the softened flesh with a spoon.

Chop the flesh finely, put it in a bowl, and mix with the lemon juice, tahini, olive oil, garlic, salt, and pepper. Serve with toasted pita or flatbread.

NUTRITION per serving:
- 151 cals • 4 g protein • 13 g fat (2 g saturates)
- 2 g carbs (2 g total sugars) • 4 g fiber

CRUDITÉS

Serve the dips with any of the following crudités:

- Florets of broccoli
- Florets of cauliflower
- Strips of red, yellow, orange, or green pepper
- Carrot sticks
- Celery sticks
- Small mushrooms
- Cherry tomatoes
- Crisp endive leaves
- Snow or sugarpeas
- Baby sweet corn
- Radishes
- Spring onions
- Cucumber, cut into strips
- Zucchini, cut into strips

Clockwise from top left:
Hummus, Guacamole,
Baba ghanoush,
Butter bean dip

AVOCADO TOAST

There are so many good things to say about avocado or "avo toast." It's so nutritious, so easy, and so simple, that it's hard to believe that a partnership of just two foods can taste so amazing. The combination of healthy fats from the avocado and carbohydrates from the toast are incredibly satiating. Avocados are also loaded with vitamin E, potassium, and folate. I prefer wholegrain toast but sourdough or rye toast also work very well.

1 slice of wholegrain toast

$^1/_2$ avocado

Optional toppings: sliced or chopped tomatoes, red pepper or chili flakes, a few chopped almonds

Serves 1

Toast the bread. In a small bowl roughly mash up the avocado and slather it on top of the toast. Sprinkle over some coarse salt and a grind of fresh black pepper. That's it!

NUTRITION per portion:
- 213 cals • 5 g protein • 14 g fat (3 g saturates)
- 15 g carbs (1 g total sugars) • 5 g fiber

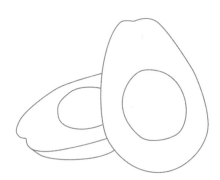

STRAWBERRY RECOVERY SHAKE

This easy-to-make smoothie contains the optimal amount of protein to promote muscle repair.

1 scoop strawberry whey protein
A handful of strawberries
¾ cup any milk of your choice
3 tbsp low-fat plain Greek yogurt
Serves 1

Blend until smooth and serve chilled.

NUTRITION per serving:
• 208 cals • 27 g protein • 1 g fat (<1 g saturates)
• 18 g carbs (18 g total sugars) • 2 g fiber

RASPBERRY CHIA RECOVERY SHAKE

The addition of the raspberries makes this shake a rich source of vitamin C, while the chia seeds supply valuable amounts of omega-3s, fiber, antioxidants, calcium, and magnesium.

½ cup raspberries
⅔ cup any milk of your choice
½ banana, sliced
⅓ cup low-fat plain Greek yogurt
1 tbsp runny honey
1 tbsp chia seeds
Optional: Crushed ice
Serves 1

Blend until smooth and serve chilled.

NUTRITION per serving:
• 303 cals • 20 g protein • 6 g fat (<1 g saturates)
• 39 g carbs (37 g total sugars) • 8 g fiber

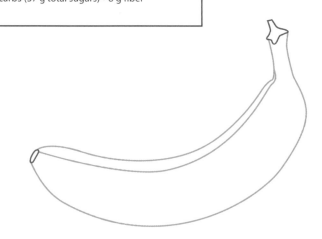

Clockwise from top right: *Berry blast smoothie, Avocado smoothie, Beet shake, Strawberry recovery shake*

BEET SHAKE

Beets are rich in nitrate, which helps improves blood flow and oxygen delivery to the muscles during exercise. Here's a tasty way to add it to your diet.

1 small raw beet, peeled and chopped

²/₃ cup fresh or frozen berries
(e.g. blueberries, strawberries, raspberries)

¹/₃ cup apple juice

¹/₃ cup low-fat plain Greek yogurt

Serves 1

Blend until smooth and serve chilled.

NUTRITION per serving:
- 243 cals • 8 g protein • 2 g fat (1 g saturates)
- 47 g carbs (39 g total sugars) • 7 g fiber

BANANA AND PEANUT BUTTER SHAKE

If you're serious about adding muscle, this smoothie is the ideal training aid.
It's packed with protein, carbs, vitamins, and minerals—and it tastes amazing!

1 banana

1 scoop vanilla or banana whey protein

1 tbsp peanut butter

1 1/4 cups any milk of your choice (or water)

Serves 1

Blend until smooth and serve chilled.

NUTRITION per serving:
- 344 cals • 32 g protein • 16 g fat (3 g saturates)
- 17 g carbs (16 g total sugars) • 3 g fiber

GREEN SMOOTHIE

This smoothie is not only a great way of getting extra green veg in your diet
but it's also loaded with vitamin C, potassium, folate, and iron.

1 1/2 cups kale or spinach

1/4 cup pineapple

1/2 banana

1 cup any milk of your choice
or low-fat yogurt

Serves 1

Blend until smooth and serve chilled.

NUTRITION per serving:
- 189 cals • 11 g protein • 2 g fat (1 g saturates)
- 30 g carbs (29 g total sugars) • 4 g fiber

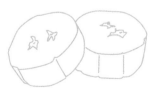

BERRY BLAST SMOOTHIE

This smoothie is ideal as a pre-workout or post-workout drink—the oats supply sustained energy and the milk and yogurt supply optimal levels of protein to hasten muscle recovery.

½ cup any milk of your choice

½ cup low-fat Greek yogurt

¾ cup mix of frozen berries e.g. blackberries, blueberries, and blackcurrants

2 tbsp rolled oats

A little runny honey

Serves 1

Blend until smooth and serve chilled.

NUTRITION per serving:
- 270 cals • 20 g protein • 2 g fat (1 g saturates)
- 41 g carbs (26 g total sugars) • 4 g fiber

STRAWBERRY AND BANANA SMOOTHIE

Perfect after a hard training session, this smoothie contains all the protein, quality carbs, and vitamins you'll need for rapid muscle recovery.

1 banana

A handful of strawberries

¾ cup any type of milk

⅓ cup low-fat Greek yogurt

Serves 1

Blend until smooth and serve chilled.

NUTRITION per serving:
- 275 cals • 20 g protein • 1 g fat (<1 g saturates)
- 1 g fat (<1 g saturates) • 3 g fiber

AVOCADO SMOOTHIE

This green smoothie is loaded with healthy monounsaturated fats, thanks to the avocado, as well as vitamin E, calcium, and iron.

$1/2$ avocado

$1/4$ cup pineapple

$1/2$ cup any milk of your choice (or pineapple juice)

A handful of spinach

$1/2$ banana

$1/2$ cup water or coconut water

Serves 1

Blend until smooth and serve chilled.

NUTRITION per serving:
• 282 cals • 7 g protein • 16 g fat (3 g saturates)
• 26 g carbs (23 g total sugars) • 6 g fiber

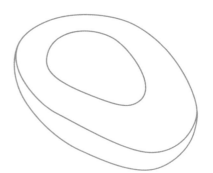

REFERENCES

Alexander, D., Ball, M. J., and Mann, J., 'Nutrient intake and haematological status of vegetarians and age-sex matched omnivores', *European Journal of Clinical Nutrition* 48 (1998), 538–46.

American Dietetic Association, 'Position of the American Dietetic Association, Dietitians of Canada, and the American College of Sports Medicine: Nutrition and Athletic Performance', *Journal of American Dietetic Association* 109 (2009), 509–27.

Appleby, P. N., Davey, G. K. and Key, T. J. 'Hypertension and blood pressure among meat eaters, fish eaters, vegetarians and vegans in EPIC-Oxford', *Public Health Nutrition* 5/5 (2002), 645–54.

Appleby, P. N., Thorogood, M., Mann, J. I. and Key, T. J., 'The Oxford Vegetarian Study: an overview', *American Journal of Clinical Nutrition* 70/3 (Suppl) (1999), 525S–531S.

Appleby, P. N., and Key T. J., 'The long-term health of vegetarians and vegans', *Proceedings of the Nutrition Society* Dec. 28, 1-7 (2015) [ePub ahead of print].

Bajželj, B., et al., 'Importance of food-demand management for climate mitigation', *Nature Climate Change* 4 (2014), 924–29.

Ball, M. J., and Bartlett, M. A., 'Dietary intake and iron status of Australian vegetarian women', *American Journal of Clinical Nutrition* 70 (1999), 353–58.

Barr, S. I., and Rideout, C. A., 'Nutritional considerations for vegetarian athletes', *Nutrition* 20/7–8 (2004), 696–703.

Bastide, N. M., et al., 'Heme Iron from Meat and Risk of Colorectal Cancer: A Meta-analysis and a Review of the Mechanisms Involved', *Cancer Prevention Research* 4 (2011), 177–84.

Bates B., et al., 'National diet and nutrition survey. Headline results from years 1, 2 and 3 (combined) of the rolling programme (2008/2009–2010/11)', (2012), https://www.gov.uk/government/uploads/system/uploads/attachment_data/file/207708/NDNS-Y3-report_All-TEXT-docs-combined.pdf [accessed March 2015].

Berners-Lee, M., et al., 'The relative greenhouse gas impacts of realistic dietary choices', *Energy Policy* 43 (2012), 184–90.

Bouvard, V., et al., 'Carcinogenicity of consumption of red and processed meat', *The Lancet Oncology* 16/16 (2015), 1599–600.

British Dietetic Association (2014), https://www.bda.uk.com/foodfacts/vegetarianfoodfacts.pdf [accessed March 2015].

Burke, D. G., Chilibeck, P. D., Parise, G., Candow, D. G., Mahoney, D. and Tarnopolsky, M., 'Effect of creatine and weight training on muscle creatine and performance in vegetarians', *Medicine and Science in Sports and Exercise* 35/11 (2003), 1946–55.

Campbell, B., Kreider, R. B., Ziegenfuss, T., et al., 'International Society of Sports Nutrition position stand: protein and exercise', *Journal of the International Society of Sports Nutrition* 4/8 (2007).

Carbon Trust, 'The Case for Protein Diversity', (2015), https://www.carbontrust.com/media/671648/the-case-for-protein-diversity.pdf [accessed March 2015].

Chan, D. S., Lau, R., Aune, D., Vieira, R., Greenwood, D. C., Kampman, E., and Norat, T., 'Red and processed meat and colorectal cancer incidence: meta-analysis of prospective studies', *PLOS ONE* 6/6 (2011), e20456.

Close, G. L., Cobley, R. J., Owens, D. J., et al., 'Assessment of vitamin D concentration in non-supplemented professional athletes and healthy adults during the winter months in the UK: implications for skeletal muscle function', *Journal of Sports Science* 31/4 (2013): 344–53.

Cockburn, E., Robson–Ansley, P., Hayes, P. R., et al., 'Effect of volume of milk consumed on the attenuation of exercise-induced muscle damage', *European Journal of Applied Physiology* 112/9 (2012), 3187–94.

Cooper, R., et al., 'Creatine supplementation with specific view to exercise/sports performance: an update', *Journal of the International Society of Sports Nutrition* 9/33 (2012).

Craddock, J., et al., 'Vegetarian and Omnivorous Nutrition - Comparing Physical Performance', *International Journal of Sport Nutrition and Exercise Metabolism* (2015), [Epub ahead of print].

Craig, W. J., Mangels, A. R., 'Position of the American Dietetic Association: vegetarian diets', *Journal of American Dietetic Association* 109/7 (2009), 1266–82.

Crowe, Francesca L., et al., 'Risk of hospitalization or death from ischemic heart disease among British vegetarians and nonvegetarians: results from the EPIC-Oxford cohort study', *American Journal of Clinical Nutrition* 97/3 (2013), 597–603.

Eating Better, 'New survey shows support for Eating Better messages' (2013), www.eating-better.org/blog/23/New-survey-showssupport-for-Eating-Better-messages.html [accessed March 2015].

Eisinger, M., 'Nutrient intake of endurance runners with lacto-ovo vegetarian diet and regular Western diet', *Z Ernahrungswiss* 33 (1994), 217–29.

Fields, H., et al. 'Is Meat Killing Us?', *Journal of American Osteopathic Association,* 116/May (2016), 296-300.

Gardner, C. D., Coulston, A., et al., 'The effect of a plant-based diet on plasma lipids in hypercholesterolemic adults: a randomized trial', *Annals of Internal Medicine* 142/9 (2005), 725–33.

Goldenburg, S., 'America's nine most wasteful fisheries named', *The Guardian* (20 March 2014).

Goodland, R. and Anhang, J., 'Livestock and Climate Change: What if the key actors in climate change were pigs, chickens and cows?' *World Watch* (2009), 10–19.

Haub, M. D., Wells, A. M., Tarnopolsky, M. A. and Campbell, W. W., 'Effect of protein source on resistive-training-induced changes in body composition and muscle size in older men', *American Journal of Clinical Nutrition* 76/3 (2002), 511–17.

Huang, R-H., et al., 'Vegetarian Diets and Weight Reduction: a Meta-Analysis of Randomized Controlled Trials', *Journal of General Internal Medicine* 31/1 (2016), 109–16.

Janelle, K. C., Barr, S. I., 'Nutrient intakes and eating behavior scores of vegetarian and nonvegetarian women'. *Journal of American Dietetic Association* 95/2 (1995), 180-6.

Jeukendrup, A. E., and Killer, S. C., 'The myths surrounding pre-exercise carbohydrate feeding', *Annals of Nutrition and Metabolism* 57 (suppl) 2 (2010), 18–25.

Key, T. J., Davey, G. K. and Appleby, P. N., 'Health benefits of a vegetarian diet', *Proceedings of the Nutrition Society* 58 (1999a), 271–75.

Key, T. J., et al., 'Mortality in vegetarians and nonvegetarians: detailed findings from a collaborative analysis of 5 prospective studies.' *American Journal of Clinical Nutrition* 70/3 (1999b) 516s-524s.

Key, T. J., Appleby, P. N., Spencer, E.A., et al., 'Cancer Incidence in Vegetarians: results from the European Prospective Investigation into Cancer and Nutrition', *American Journal Clinical Nutrition* 89/5 (2009), 1620S–26S.

Larsson, S. C., and Wolk, A., 'Meat consumption and risk of colorectal cancer: A meta-analysis of prospective studies', *International Journal of Cancer* 119 (2006), 2657–64.

Lassale, C., Beulens, J., Van der Schouw, Y., et al., 'A Pro-Vegetarian Food Pattern and Cardiovascular Mortality in the Epic Study', *Circulation* 131 (Suppl 1) (2015), A16-A16.

Le, L. T., and Sabaté, J., 'Beyond Meatless, the Health Effects of Vegan Diets: Findings from the Adventist Cohorts', *Nutrients* 6/6 (2014), 2131–47.

Maffucci, D. M., and McMurray, R. G., 'Towards optimizing the timing of the pre-exercise meal', *International Journal of Sport Nutrition and Exercise Metabolism* 10/2 (2000), 103–13.

Moore, D. R., Areta, J., Coffey, V. J., et al., 'Daytime pattern of post-exercise protein intake affects whole-body protein turnover in resistance-trained males', *Nutrition & Metabolism* 9/91 (2012).

Moore, D. R., Robinson, M. J., Fry, J. L., et al., 'Ingested protein dose response of muscle and albumin protein synthesis after resistance exercise in young men', *American Journal of Clinical Nutrition* 89 (2009), 161–68.

Nieman, D. C., 'Physical fitness and vegetarian diets: is there a relation?', *American Journal of Clinical Nutrition* 70/3 (1999), 570S–575S.

Norat, T., et al. 'Meat, fish, and colorectal cancer risk: the European prospective investigation into cancer and nutrition,' *Journal of the National Cancer Institute* 97 (2005), 906–16.

Orlich, M. J., Singh, P., Sabaté, J., et al. 'Vegetarian Dietary Patterns and Mortality in Adventist Health Study 2' *JAMA Internal Medicine* 173/13 (2013), 1230–238.

Pettersen, B. J., Anousheh, R., Fan, J., Jaceldo-Siegl, K. and Fraser, G. E., 'Vegetarian diets and blood pressure among white subjects: Results from the Adventist Health Study-2 (AHS-2)', *Public Health Nutrition* 15 (2012), 1909–16.

Phillips, S. M., and Van Loon, L. J., 'Dietary protein for athletes: from requirements to optimum adaptation', *Journal of Sports Science* 29/ Suppl 1 (2011), S29–38.

Phillips, S. M., Moore, D. R., Tang, J. E., et al., 'A critical examination of dietary protein requirements, benefits and excesses in athletes', *International Journal of Sports Nutrition and Exercise Metabolism* 17 (2007), 58–78.

Pimentel, D., and Pimentel, M., 'Sustainability of meat-based and plant-based diets and the environment', *American Journal of Clinical Nutrition* 78/3 (2003), 660S–63S.

Pimentel, D., et al., 'Water Resources: Agricultural and Environmental Issues', *BioScience* 54/10 (2004), 909-918.

Richter, E. A., 'Immune parameters in male athletes after a lacto-ovo vegetarian diet and a mixed Western diet', *Medicine and Science in Sports Exercise,* 23/5 (1991), 517-21.

Rodriguez, N. R., DiMarco, N. M., Langley, S., et al., 'Position of the American Dietetic Association, Dietitians of Canada, and the American College of Sports Medicine: Nutrition and athletic performance', *Journal of American Dietetic Association* 100 (2009), 1543–1556.

Rohrmann, S., et al., 'Meat consumption and mortality: results from the European Prospective Investigation into Cancer and Nutrition', *BMC Medicine* 11 (2013), 11/63.

SACN. 'Iron and Health', Department of Health: Scientific Advisory Committee on Nutrition 2010. (London).

Sánchez-Villegas, A. et al., 'A longitudinal analysis of diet quality scores and the risk of incident depression in the SUN Project', *BMC Medicine* 2015, 13:197.

Scarborough, P. et al. 'Dietary greenhouse gas emissions of meat-eaters, fish-eaters, vegetarians and vegans in the UK', *Climatic Change* 125/2 (2014), 179–92.

Singh, P. N., Sabaté, J. and Fraser, G. E., 'Does low meat consumption increase life expectancy in humans?' *American Journal of Clinical Nutrition* 78/3 Suppl (2003), 526S–32S.

Snowdon, D. A., 'Animal product consumption and mortality

because of all causes combined, coronary heart disease, stroke, diabetes, and cancer in Seventh-day Adventists.' *American Journal of Clinical Nutrition* 48/3 (1988), 739–48.

Snyder A. C., Dvorak L. L., Roepke J. B., 'Influence of dietary iron source on measures of iron status among female runners', *Medicine & Science in Sports Exercise* 21 (1989), 7–10.

Song, Y., Manson, J. E., Buring, J. E. and Liu, S. L., 'A prospective study of red meat consumption and type 2 diabetes in middle-aged and elderly women', *Diabetes Care* 27 (2004), 2108–15.

Soret, S., et al., 'Climate change mitigation and health effects of varied dietary patterns in real-life settings throughout North America', *American Journal of Clinical Nutrition* 1000/Suppl 1 (2014), 490S–95S.

Spector, T., *The Diet Myth: The real science behind what we eat.* London: W & N (2015).

Spencer, E. A., Appleby, P. N., Davey, G. K. and Key, T. J., 'Weight gain over 5 years in 21,966 meat-eating, fish-eating, vegetarian, and vegan men and women in EPIC-Oxford', *International Journal of Obesity and Related Metabolic Disorders* 27/6 (2003), 728–34.

Springmann, M., et al., 'Analysis and valuation of the health and climate change co-benefits of dietary change', *PNAS*, 113/15 (2016), 4146–4151.

Tonstad, S., Butler, T., Yan, R., Fraser, G., 'Type of vegetarian diet, body weight and prevalence of type 2 diabetes', *Diabetes Care* 32 (2009), 791–96.

Tonstad, S., Stewart, K., Oda, K., Batech, M., Herring, R. P. and Fraser, G. E., 'Vegetarian diets and incidence of diabetes in the Adventist Health Study-2', *Nutrition, Metabolism and Cardiovascular Disorder* 23/4 (2013), 292–99.

Venderley, A. M., and Campbell, W. W., 'Vegetarian diets. Nutritional considerations for athletes', *Sports Medicine* 36 (2006), 295–305.

WCRF/AICR, 'Food, Nutrition, Physical Activity, and the Prevention of Cancer: a Global Perspective', (2007).

Williams M. H., *Nutritional aspects of human physical and athletic performance.* Springfield, IL: Charles C Thomas Publisher Ltd (1985), 415–6.

Welch, A. A., et al., 'Dietary intake and status of n-3 polyunsaturated fatty acids in a population of fish-eating and non-fish-eating meat-eaters, vegetarians, and vegans and the precursor-product ratio of alpha-linolenic acid to long-chain n-3 polyunsaturated fatty acids: results from the EPIC-Norfolk cohort.' *American Journal of Clinical Nutrition* 92/5 (2010), 1040–51.

Wellesley, L., et al., 'Changing Climate, Changing Diets Pathways to Lower Meat Consumption', *Chatham House Report* (2015).

Young V. R. and Pellett P. L., 'Plant proteins in relation to human protein and amino acid nutrition', *American Journal of Clinical Nutrition* 59 (suppl) (1994), 1203S-1212S.

RESOURCES

www.cowspiracy.com The website of the feature-length documentary, *Cowspiracy: The Sustainability Secret*, provides facts and resources behind the film on the impact of animal agriculture on the environment.

www.ewg.org/meateatersguide The website of the Environmental Working Group and the report, 'The Meat Eater's Guide to Climate Change and Health', provides information about meat consumption and the environment.

www.vegsoc.org The website of the UK Vegetarian Society provides clear information and fact sheets on health and nutrition, animal welfare, sustainability, the environment, and recipes.

www.vegansociety.com The website of the UK Vegan Society provides comprehensive resources on the vegan lifestyle, nutrition, food, the environment as well as many recipes.

www.savvyvegetarian.com This US website provides useful articles and advice on vegetarian and vegan diet and nutrition, health,

cooking, environmental issues, green living, sustainability, and related issues.

www.vrg.org The US Vegetarian Resource Group provides information on vegetarian and vegan nutrition, recipes, ingredients, and vegetarian restaurants and some useful articles for vegetarian athletes.

www.ausport.gov.au/ais The Australian Institute of Sport provides authoritative fact sheets on vegetarian eating and sports nutrition.

www.nomeatathlete.com This website of marathon runner and author Matt Frazier provides articles and resources for vegetarian athletes.

www.veganhealth.org This US website written by a registered dietitian has in-depth articles on vegan nutrition and vegan meal plans.

INDEX